Anna S. Bushby

The Danes:

Sketched by themselves; a series of popular stories by the best Danish authors -

Vol. 2

Anna S. Bushby

The Danes:
Sketched by themselves; a series of popular stories by the best Danish authors - Vol. 2

ISBN/EAN: 9783337723910

Printed in Europe, USA, Canada, Australia, Japan

Cover: Foto ©ninafisch / pixelio.de

More available books at **www.hansebooks.com**

THE DANES

Sketched by Themselves.

A SERIES OF POPULAR STORIES BY THE BEST
DANISH AUTHORS.

TRANSLATED BY MRS. BUSHBY.

IN THREE VOLUMES.—VOL. II.

LONDON:
RICHARD BENTLEY, NEW BURLINGTON STREET.
1864.

[*The right of Translation is reserved.*]

LONDON: PRINTED BY W. CLOWES AND SONS, STAMFORD STREET,
AND CHARING CROSS.

CONTENTS OF VOL. II.

	PAGE
Too Old.—By Carit Etlar	1
Aunt Francisca.—By Carl Bernhard	49
The Shipwrecked Mariner's Treasure.—By Carit Etlar	147
Damon and Pythias.—By Carl Bernhard	221
The Fatal Chain. — From the Swedish of Uncle Adam	263

THE DANES

Sketched by Themselves.

TOO OLD.*

FROM THE DANISH OF CARIT ETLAR.

CHAPTER I.

BETWEEN Fredericia and Snoghöi the sandy and stony shore forms a tolerably broad tongue of land, which is called Lyngspoint. The coast stretches out long and flat, without any defence against the sea except a stone wall, and the fishermen who dwell here seem to have thought of nothing but the safe little bays that, on either side of the promontory, afford shelter to their small skiffs and protect them from the wild waves, and the blocks of ice

---

* "*Too Old*"—"For gammel"—is from a Danish work entitled "Haablös"—"*Hopeless*"—by Carit Etlar. The volume, which contains three tales, was published in Copenhagen in 1857.

which during winter the north-west winds drive in from the Kattegat.

Farther up on the land, the bare, desolate-looking plain of sand disappears by degrees under high banks which are overgrown by a thick, low copse of brushwood, with some stunted oak and beech-trees showing themselves as sad mementoes of an extensive wood, that formerly joined the forest of Erizö, and in the midst of which the village of Hannerup was situated. The village and the wood have both disappeared long since.

Far in among the bushes people sometimes stumble upon pieces of broken stones with their mouldering cement of lime, the last fragments of the work and walls of ages gone by: in a few years the copse itself will have vanished, and the blackbird and the thrush, whose blithe carols on the summer evenings were heard even by those sailing near in the Belt, will seek other leafy homes.

At a little distance from the sea-shore at Lyngspoint stand ten or twelve small cottages, built in the irregular style which is always observable in the houses of the peasantry of ancient days, and composed of hard clay framework and thatched roofs. To each cottage there belongs a small garden enclosed by a low earthen dyke, or a hedge of elderberries and the blackthorn. Behind several of them are to be seen boats turned upside down, lying in the sand with their keels exposed, and each furnished with a little gate in the stern. These boats serve as a shelter for sheep, or geese, after having become too frail any longer to carry their owners out to sea. The inhabitants of Lyngspoint are fishermen, a reserved and silent race, rough and stern like the element on which they pass so much of their time. Among them the struggles of life have no cessation—labour has no reward—time affords no day of rest, except when storms forbid them to launch their boats, or the sea is covered with ice; but such dreaded and unwelcome repose is always associated with distress and want. The women employ themselves in their household affairs, and not unfrequently share the labour of the men, as they always share their privations. Even the ocean's tempests are felt in common here, since every squall in which the boats are exposed to danger on the water, causes gloom and anxiety to those in the huts, who dread to lose their relatives and their means of support.

In one of these fishermen's cottages one evening

there were two persons—an old man, tall and athletic, his grey hair thin and sunburnt, his countenance decided and daring, and a woman, very youthful-looking, pale, and apparently unhappy, but nevertheless of rare beauty. He sat at a table, which was lighted by a lamp suspended by a chain from a beam in the roof, and the glare from which fell upon two long Spanish cavalry pistols which he was busy loading. She was standing at the window gazing through the dark window-panes.

It was a gloomy November evening. The storm from the seaward swept wildly along, howling dismally, while the rain beat heavily against the windows, and the flame in the lamp fluttered and flickered in the gusts of wind that rushed into the room through the open chimney. There had been a long and unbroken silence between the two occupants of the apartment; the man, while continuing his work, cast several glances towards the young woman, but always looked quickly away when she turned towards him.

At length he asked, 'At what are you looking?'

'At the weather,' she replied. 'It will be a bad night to go to sea in.'

'The weather is good enough,' he muttered,

gruffly. 'It is all the better for being dark; the darkness will be of use to us.'

So saying, he started up, buckled on a cutlass, and stuck the pistols in his belt.

'Give me something to eat.'

The woman spread the table for supper, and taking a pot off the fire, poured its contents into a dish, which she placed before the man.

There was again complete silence; he ate his supper without saying a word, while the young woman sat leaning back in her chair near the table, and fixed her eye on him with a sad, yet scrutinizing look.

'I am done,' he exclaimed, after a little while, 'and now, good-by.'

'Are you going already?' she asked, sorrowfully.

'To be sure I am—it is the time agreed on, and they will be waiting for me on the shore down yonder.'

He drew on a thick sailor's jacket over his other clothes, and went towards the door.

'Farewell, Christine!' he said, without even turning to look at her,

Christine stretched both her hands towards him, and her trembling lips moved, but the words she would have spoken died away in a deep sigh. The man turned round and walked back a step or two. For a few moments he stood in silent surprise, and then exclaimed, 'What are you weeping for?'

'Oh, Jan Steffens!' she whispered, half aloud, as she again stretched her hands towards him, 'I am so afraid lest any evil should happen to you.'

The man did not take her proffered hand, and his thick eyebrows were knitted together, as he said, 'How childish you are, Christine! What is there for you to be afraid of? I am going on a lawful errand, and things must take their course. Take care to put the fire out, and don't forget to feed the watch-dog in the morning. I have locked him up in the wash-house, that he might not make a noise to-night.'

So saying he turned to go, but when he had reached the door he came back once again, and exclaimed, with solemnity, 'May the Lord's protecting hand be over you, Christine!' In another moment he was gone.

The young woman laid her head on the table, covered her face with her hands, and wept bitterly. She had sat there for some time absorbed in grief, when suddenly she raised her head, for she had heard steps on the outside of the cottage. She got up and went to the window. Presently she saw a figure in the doorway. It was that of a young man in a sailor's dress, and armed in the same manner as Jan was.

'Good evening, dear Christine!' he exclaimed. 'Has Jan gone?'

'Yes,' she answered; 'you will find him down yonder with the other boatmen.'

The fisherman seemed to be reflecting on something, while he fixed his eyes intently upon the young woman's face. He observed that there were tears in her eyes, and approaching her, he seized her hand.

'Christine!' he exclaimed, in a soft and sympathizing voice, 'you have been weeping? Has there been any quarrel between you and your husband?'

'No,' she replied, 'there never has been any.' And as she spoke she tried to draw her hand away, but he grasped it more firmly.

'Would to Heaven you had never seen that old Jan Steffens,' he whispered; 'you would have been much happier—oh, what misery we would both have escaped!'

'Would to Heaven I had never seen you, Kjeld,' she answered; 'then, perhaps, Jan and I might have been comfortable together.'

The young fisherman's eyes sparkled at this imprudent confession, which admitted so much more than Christine had any intention of doing.

'But what harm have I done?' he asked, gently. 'We loved each other from our childish days, when we used to go to school together. Ah! *then* we looked forward to living together, to working together, to trying our luck together—and—being so happy! Then came Jan Steffens—and now—'

'And now I am Jan Steffens's wife,' cried Christine, interrupting him impetuously. 'Never speak to me more of the past, therefore, Kjeld—it is gone! It is forgotten,' she added, in a lower and sadder tone.

At that moment the light from the lamp fell upon a face, which, on the outside of the house, was intently looking in through the window. Those in the room did not observe it, and had no suspicion that prying eyes were upon them. Kjeld asked, with warmth, 'Why should we not speak of the past? We have always been only like brother and sister to each other.'

'Brother and sister!' said Christine, trying to smile, 'what else could we have been? But I am a married woman, Kjeld, and you, like every one else, are only a stranger to me. Therefore you must not come here so often—people remark the frequency of your visits, and talk of them.'

'But Jan himself has allowed them,' said the fisherman. 'Only yesterday, when we were coming from church, he asked me where I had been all last week, and why I had never once entered his house. He said that you had been speaking of me.' Christine raised her head, and cast a surprised and inquiring look at Kjeld. He went on: 'Jan said that you were longing to see me again.'

'I cannot understand his conduct,' murmured Christine, musingly.

'When your husband spoke thus,' said Kjeld, tenderly, 'why will you be harsher than he? Answer me, Christine—why may I not come here as hitherto? I ask for nothing more.'

The young woman's lips quivered, and her whole frame trembled with emotion, which she seemed struggling to overcome, as she replied, in a broken voice, 'Oh, Kjeld, leave off such questions. It is a sin on your part to speak in this manner to me.

Go—go, I beseech you. Jan will expect to meet you down yonder with the other boatmen.'

Kjeld seemed lost in thought for a few moments; he then came close to Christine, laid his hand on her head, and tried to speak—but words failed him, and turning suddenly away, he rushed from the cottage. At the same moment the face vanished, which, from the outside of the window, had been watching the scene within.

The storm appeared to be increasing. The lamp swung, and its light fluttered in the draughts of air from the ill-secured window-frames. When Christine found that she was alone, she crouched down close to the door, as if she wished to catch the last expiring echo of the footsteps of him who had just gone. She listened, but nothing was to be heard save the roaring of the tempest, and the sound of the rain pattering against the windows.

This is a tale of the year 1808, at the commencement of that unfortunate period when Denmark, without a fleet, without an army, and almost without finances, entered into war both with Sweden and England.

Down at the shore, in one of the little bays before mentioned, the water from which was conveyed a good way inland by a broad channel that had been dug for the purpose, there lay that evening two gunboats, which a number of men were getting out into the open sea. They worked hurriedly and silently, and the little noise that they unvoidably made was drowned in the roaring of the waves, which were dashing furiously on the beach of the narrow tongue of land. The men were all armed in the same way as Jan Steffens, and seemed to obey his orders.

Jan was the principal pilot of the place, and well known as an excellent seaman. The two gunboats had been built and rigged at Fredericia, and afterwards placed under his command. They were the masters of the whole Belt, so to speak, and the previous summer they had taken several valuable prizes from the English.

At the moment in question the pilot was standing on a rock on the beach, and dividing his attention between the men's work and the black clouds above, from which the rain was pouring down in torrents. All the preparations, so energetically carried on that evening, were made for the purpose of taking by surprise an English corvette, which, for want of a pilot, had anchored in a bay near Fyen shortly before the darkness and the storm had commenced.

Just about the time that the gunboats had been hauled out to the extremity of the point, two persons approached the shore, both coming from the direction of the cottages. One was a half-grown lad, the other was Kjeld. The boy looked about for the pilot, and when he perceived him standing on the rock he hastened towards him.

Jan stooped and whispered in the boy's ear,

'Was he in yonder?'

'Yes.'

'You are sure you saw him—you have not made any mistake?'

'I saw him as plainly as I now see you, Jan Steffens.'

'Very well, Jens; you can go home. Let the sails alone!' he cried, shortly after, turning towards the group of men near; 'the storm is increasing, the wind is right against us, and we must row the boats out. How late may it be, I wonder?'

'It is not yet midnight,' replied Kjeld, who had just approached the pilot. 'As I was coming along I heard the clock at Erizö church strike eleven.'

'Mongens Dal, at Fyensland, promised to place

a light in his window at twelve o'clock,' observed another. 'His farm lies close by the bay where the English ship has anchored; we have only, then, to look out for that light, and there will be no mistake.'

'Ay, ay—all right,' replied Jan, gruffly. 'Mind your own business, Vextel, and leave me to determine how we shall steer.'

A few minutes afterwards he announced that it was time for them to put to sea.

'Take your places,' cried Jan, 'and see that you make as little noise with the oars as possible. Ebbe, take the helm of the other boat, and follow close to the one I steer. We shall be a tolerable number this time, I think.'

'You promised to take the porpoise-hunters from Middlefart with us.'

'To be sure I did, and we shall find room for them; they are fine brave fellows, these porpoise-hunters. Has Kjeld come on board?'

'Yes, pilot,' answered the young man from the first gunboat.

'A word with you, Kjeld. Come a little way on shore.'

Kjeld sprang out of the boat, the pilot went up

to him, and they walked together from the beach towards the sandhills.

'You will see that Kjeld will be half-mad this evening,' said one of the seamen in the first boat. 'Jan Steffens looks as sulky and savage as can be; very likely he has found out the love affair at home in his house up yonder.'

'Poor man!' said another, 'why did he take so young a wife. He is much too old for her.'

In the meantime, after Jan and Kjeld had walked to some distance in silence side by side, Jan asked suddenly,—

'Where were you this evening, Kjeld? It was very late before you joined us.'

Kjeld stammered some almost unintelligible words, while he seemed to be framing an answer.

'You are thinking what you can say,' exclaimed the old pilot, in a voice unsteady with suppressed anger, 'for you dare not speak it out. You were with Christine. You ought not to conceal this from me. You were there also yesterday, and on Sunday, and last Friday; and, in short, whenever I am absent, at sea in my boat, or elsewhere, you find some pretext to visit her.'

'I admit it is true,' replied Kjeld, who was

startled by the stern coldness of Jan's looks and words.

'But did it never occur to you that you were wrong in visiting her so often? Christine is a married woman, and you will bring discredit upon her with your frequent visits.'

'I am a man of honour, Jan Steffens,' replied Kjeld, in a voice that trembled somewhat with anxiety at what might be the result of this conversation, 'and I have never behaved in your house in any way that you or the whole world might not have witnessed.'

'That is, perhaps, a misfortune, sir.'

'A misfortune!' exclaimed Kjeld, in amazement; 'what can you mean?'

'If it had been otherwise,' replied Jan, quietly, 'I should have put a pistol to your head, and shot you—that's all. It would have been better both for you and her, maybe.'

'But you yourself gave me permission to visit at your house; you said that Christine longed to have some news of me.'

'Well, if I said that, of course you knew on whose account I asked you to come. You need not take the matter so much to heart, my lad; let us speak reasonably now. I know that you are a well-principled young man, Kjeld; I have watched you narrowly ever since Christine and I were married. I am aware how things stand between you two; I know all, Kjeld!'

'You?'

'Ah, yes! I know that she loves you, and that she has never in her life cared for anyone else.'

'Then you know, also, that I am the most unfortunate man on earth,' replied Kjeld.

'You!' exclaimed Jan, shrugging up his shoulders mockingly—'you! No, my lad, there is one who beats you in misfortune.'

'Who?'

'*I*. If you had acted towards me as you ought to have done, you would have come to me when I was courting Christine, and have told me how things were between you and her.'

'We thought of doing that, Jan Steffens, but we did not dare to risk it.'

'Nonsense—nonsense! one should dare everything to fulfil one's duty. But you kept silence at that time, so did she, and matters were allowed to take their course.'

'Oh, Jan Steffens!' replied the young fisherman,

in a voice trembling with emotion, 'what could I have said to you? I was a poor fellow, working hard to obtain food enough for my own support. You were well off, and had been kind to Christine's father, therefore they were glad to let you have the girl.'

'A very good reason, truly. What! because I had been kind to the old people, had I a claim to make their daughter unhappy? No; the blame was your own. You both kept silence, and yourselves are answerable for the evil that followed. Hearken, Kjeld! from this evening forward we must understand each other. I loved Christine from the first moment I beheld her; she was so amiable, so dutiful, and so full of affectionate feeling for the old people, her parents, and so attentive to them, that I thought she would make an excellent wife. I knew that she would have many more comforts in my house than she had at home. I reflected on everything, except upon the difference between our ages. She was silent—she wept; but she married me. Since that time, Kjeld, I have done all that a man could do to make myself liked. I was kind and indulgent to her. I allowed her to rule in all things, and to do whatever she pleased. I brought her home the most beautiful dresses and presents when I went on voyages. But all was of no avail. I was *too old*.

'I bought a new boat for her father, I took her mother into our house, I clothed her little sisters and sent them to school, I prayed to the Lord every morning and evening of my life in mercy to inspire her with kindly feelings towards me—but in vain, in vain! She went through her duties, and was civil and good-tempered; but love me she never could. When I was young, like you, Kjeld, I dared not attach myself to any woman, because I was *too poor;* now that I have become rich, none will attach herself to me, because I am *too old*. You look sad. Ah, so goes the world, my boy! It was not long before I found out that you loved Christine; and, alas! still worse—I too soon perceived how much she cared for you. While you both thought the secret was buried in your own hearts, I read it as if in an open book. Then I was seized with the most furious jealousy. I resolved to murder you, and more than once, at that period, there was but a hair-breadth between you and death. I watched you closely—my eyes were often on you, and never were you out of my thoughts.'

Jan stopped; he seemed to be nerving himself to

go on with his narration. Kjeld observed that he was shaking, as if in an ague fit.

'You were an honourable man, Kjeld, as you declared a little while ago,' continued Jan, 'yet that which ought to have made my unhappiness less, absolutely added to it. I have nothing to complain of—nothing to reproach you with—all falls back upon myself—upon that disastrous, that wretched union of hands, in which the soul took no part; and when one has come to the full knowledge that such was the case, the painful truth fastens itself upon the mind, and impels one to seek some remedy to the misfortune.'

'You are right, Jan Steffens,' replied Kjeld, earnestly. 'I, too, have been reflecting upon a remedy since I left Christine a little while ago, when she wished to Heaven she had never known me—never even beheld me.'

'Did Christine really say that?' exclaimed the pilot with surprise, but, it must be owned, not without feeling somewhat pleased and flattered. 'Well, that was rather a cruel wish to bestow on you this evening, when she thought that you were going on an expedition from whence many of us will, perhaps, never return.'

'Christine is a better wife than you fancy; she discards every thought that is not in accordance with her duty; I shall not be wanting in mine either, and I have hit upon a plan to set all to rights.'

'So have I,' said the pilot.

'I shall go away and engage myself on board some ship trading with a foreign country, and neither she nor you shall see me often again, if it shall please God to spare my life in our enterprise to-night.'

'That he certainly will do, my lad, for a good reason—that you shall not go with us.'

'Not go with you! What do you mean by that?' asked Kjeld, in the utmost amazement.

'Listen!' replied Jan, with cold, quiet decision of manner. 'I have not much time to spare, and my resolution is taken. Because you have behaved honourably, and because you have both felt so kindly disposed towards an old man who, without knowing or intending it, brought upon you the greatest disappointment that can befall anyone, I will ensure you both a reward. Go back to Christine, and tell her, that from this evening henceforth I will bestow on her all the liberty she can desire; she shall no longer have cause to grieve and to weep, as she has so often done when she supposed no one saw her, or at night, when she thought I was asleep: you can say that since it was impossible for me to win her affection, and be happy myself, I will not hinder her from being so. On this account, it is not *you*, young man, but *I*, who must go away to a distant land, never more to return.'

It would be difficult to describe the young seaman's amazement as he listened to these words.

'I do not at all understand you, Jan Steffens,' he said. 'What do you mean by speaking in this manner?'

'They are calling to me from the boats!' cried Jan. 'Do you not hear their shouts? I must away. What do I mean?' he added, in a lower tone. 'It is easily understood; if I die to-night, I cannot stand in your way to-morrow.'

'Die!' cried Kjeld. 'Are you going to kill yourself?'

'No,' replied the pilot, calmly. 'But I feel pretty sure that the Englishmen will take the trouble of despatching me upon themselves.'

'No, no! that shall not be! You must let me

go with you, Jan Steffens, and share your danger; you promised that you would. Besides, according to the lots that we drew in the dark, I have a right to accompany you. And if you were to die—if you were to put yourself forward to be killed—I should be still more miserable than I am now. Christine would never be mine, if that happiness were purchased by your death to-night.'

'Oh, as to that, you will change your tune when the time comes,' replied the pilot, turning to go; but Kjeld stopped him, and placing himself before him, while he seized his arms, exclaimed,

'Oh, Jan Steffens! take me with you; I entreat you, as the greatest favour, to do so. You shall not forsake Christine; you are a far better husband to her than I should be. Let me go with the boats!'

Jan shook himself free from the young man's grasp, and in answer to his earnest appeal, he said,

'It shall be as I have determined, Kjeld, so there is no use for another word on the subject. But you must not go to Christine till to-morow, for you may well believe that I must have ceased to live before I cease to love her. Farewell, Kjeld— be kind to her, and make her as happy as you can.

She is very mild, and is easily intimidated. When she is yours, and you speak of me in future years, remember that I wished to do good to you both—that I atoned for my fault as well as I could—and that my greatest misfortune was—that she was so young, or rather, that I was *too old*.'

The pilot wrung Kjeld's hand as he said these words, and before the young fisherman had time to conquer his emotion so as to be able to make any reply, the old man had left him, and was crossing the sand with rapid strides towards the shore where the boats' crews were assembled. Kjeld followed him, crying, 'Jan Steffens, let me go with you only this once; do not thus turn a deaf ear to me. You will rob me of my honour, my share in your glory, if I alone am to be left behind.'

'Push off!' shouted the pilot, as he jumped into the leading gunboat, and took his place at the helm.

The oars sank, and both the boats began to move towards the sea. Kjeld uttered a despairing cry, and sprang after them, but he could not reach them, and the waves cast him back on the shore.

'Things shall be as I have said,' he heard in the pilot's deep voice from the foremost boat. 'But do not go up yonder before to-morrow, and may the Lord be with you both!'

The men in the boats had been astonished witnesses of this scene. Those who sat nearest to him cast looks of inquiry towards the pilot; but his eye gave no responsive glance, his sunburnt face only expressed inflexible resolution, and his countenance was, perhaps, a little sterner even than usual.

From the beach Kjeld saw the boats rising and sinking amidst the foaming waves, while his passionate entreaties and his wild shouts were lost in the roaring of the wind and the thunder of the sea. The rain was pouring in torrents, and the skies were obscured by heavy black clouds. Soon after the two boats appeared only as dark specks upon the water, and presently even these vanished amidst the thick fog which rested over the sea at a little distance.

Fortunately the current was running northwards that night—that is to say, in a direction which favoured the progress of the gunboats, so that their crews were not obliged to fatigue themselves with rowing hard. The raging sea broke repeatedly over the boats, but no one seemed to mind this;

they placed complete confidence in the pilot, whose tall figure, apparently immovable, stood upright at the helm: and perhaps the thoughts of all were directed to the object of their expedition, which they were rapidly approaching. The rain had somewhat abated in that particular place, and when a gust of wind partially dispelled the fog for a moment, they saw on the opposite high coast of Fyen the signal-light, which, though it was but faint and flickering, pointed out to them where they should seek the enemy. Amidst the profound silence that reigned in the boats, the pilot addressed the men in low but distinct tones.

'Row more quietly still, Gutter! Make no noise with your oars; you may be certain that they have their eyes and ears open yonder. They know right well where they are. Have the guns clear in front there, Nikolai; you must show us to-night that you understand your work like an old artilleryman. The wind will fall off the nearer we come under the shelter of the hilly land. If I see aright, we have our man there in the lee of the boats.'

All eyes were instantly turned in the direction he had named; a dark object became soon after perceptible amidst the thick gloom around, it gradually grew in size and developed its outline, until the hull of a ship was to be discerned, sharp and black, reposing on the waters like a swan.

CHAPTER II.

In pursuance of the plan which Jan Steffens had arranged, the boats shaped their course so as to come between the land and the corvette. They could hear the wind whistling amidst the cordage, could see the light in the captain's cabin, and the heads of the officers of the watch as they paced up and down the quarter-deck. The silence which had reigned on board was broken the moment the pilot's boat was perceived from the ship. Immediately afterwards Jan's sonorous voice was heard commanding his men to fire. Both the gunboats fired at the same moment, and with terrible effect.

It would be in vain to try to describe the commotion which now took place on board the enemy's ship. The attack had been made as suddenly as it had been planned; it was also favoured in the highest degree by the darkness and the tempest, which embarrassed many of the movements of the ship at anchor, whilst the gunboats, on the contrary, were able to move easily towards the places where their fire would operate most effectively, and be most destructive. Under these fortunate circumstances the fishermen continued to load and to discharge their guns. Splinters and pieces of broken planks evinced the accuracy of their gunners. On board the corvette they were not able to point their cannon so low that they could sweep the boats, whose flat hulls, besides, were only visible during the flashes of fire from the guns, and in an instant after seemed to have been swallowed up by the lofty billows.

Meanwhile the drums beat on board the ship; the boatswain's whistle mingled with the officer's words of command—disorder was at an end. Everything was done that circumstances permitted to oppose the enemy, and their fire was returned whenever their position could be ascertained. Soon after the rain ceased, and faint rays of pale moonlight struggled through the dark masses of clouds that were driving across the skies. The gunboats came close under the man-of-war, and after another discharge of their guns, the crews boarded the ship, climbing in by every possible opening, amidst cries of joyous triumph; and then commenced a scene in which were mingled the sounds of oaths, shouts, and pistol-shots, while everything was shrouded in the thick veil of mist and dark clouds of smoke.

At Lyngspoint every shot was heard, and caused the deepest anxiety for the absent. As usual upon similar occasions, lights appeared in all the fishermen's huts. None of the females thought of sleep while their husbands and their brothers were fighting upon the stormy sea. The tempest roared around the cottages, the watch-dogs howled as if lamenting their masters' danger, and the crowing of the cocks announced the approach of morning. Pale countenances, expressive of fear and anxiety, appeared one after the other at the half-open doors; presently the women began to go over to each other's houses to communicate their forebodings, or to seek for the comfort so much needed. In the little porch of one of the houses nearest to the shore stood a group of three females muffled up in woollen shawls and gazing upon the sea. Every shot was noticed by them with a sigh or a speaking glance.

'There is warm work going on over yonder,' groaned one woman.

'Ah, yes!' replied another; 'I was just thinking that every one of these shots may cost a man's life—the lives of *our* men, perhaps.'

'Nonsense! there is nothing to make such a fuss about,' exclaimed a rough voice. 'Our people's lives are in God's hands, even though they may stand before the barrel of a gun, or ride on a plank over the ocean. I have put up a prayer to the Lord for my boy. "Do your duty," I said to him when he went away, "and our Almighty Father will order the rest as seems good to Him!"'

She who spoke thus was an extraordinary-looking woman. Her face was entirely covered with wrinkles and marks of the small-pox, which made her harsh features look still coarser than they really were. Some years before the date of the night in question, her husband had been lost at sea, and she and her little son had been left in the utmost poverty. From that time Ellen went out with the men to fish: she worked as hard as the best of them, managed her boat like an experienced seaman, and never seemed to feel fatigue. Equipped in a short dress, a pair of large fisherman's boots, and a dark, low hat, which in nautical language is called 'a sou'-wester,' she was to be seen in the worst weather carrying her fish about to the neigh bouring farms for sale; in the autumn months she hired the old right of ferryman at Snoghöi, and carried fruit over from Æro to Zealand—she took travellers across to Strib—mended her own boat when it needed repairs; in short, she worked hard, for she worked to maintain her son.

Doubtless some local readers of this slight sketch will recognize in Ellen an old acquaintance, who was always welcome wherever she showed herself; an honest, upright, self-sacrificing character, whose whole life was one scene of unflinching devotion to her duties, until she suddenly disappeared from her home, and was never seen again.

Ellen was standing with a short clay-pipe in her mouth, her rough grey locks confined by a handkerchief tied under her chin.

'I'll tell you what, Ellen,' said one of the other women, 'let us run over to Stine Steffens, as none of us have any mind to go to sleep to-night. She has a warm, comfortable room, and can give us a good cup of coffee.'

Her proposition was readily agreed to by the group of women who had now assembled, and, tying handkerchiefs over their heads like hoods, they all repaired to Jan Steffens's house, with the exception of 'Skipper Ellen,' as she was generally called, who remained behind.

Christine was still sitting in the same corner of the room where she had placed herself after Kjeld had left her. Her beautiful, expressive eyes were swimming in tears.

'Good evening, little Stine!' cried one of the fisherwomen. 'How goes it with you?'

'Oh, as with the rest of you,' she replied. 'I am full of anxiety and terror. It was kind of you to come here. Pray sit down.'

'You had better come to one of our houses, and we shall make some good strong coffee; that will help to kill the time.'

'We can make the coffee as well here,' said Christine.

'Oh, certainly,' said the other, joyfully, 'and I will help to blow up the fire.'

The fire was rekindled, the coffee made, and the conversation was then resumed.

'Would to Heaven our people were safe at home again!' exclaimed Christine. 'I am so terrified at the risk they are running to-night.'

'And with good reason too,' said one of the women. 'There is sure to be sorrow among some of us to-morrow, for the firing has been going on at least half-an-hour. But we must comfort ourselves by remembering that storm and sunshine come from the same hand; and if some are sufferers others will be gainers, for no doubt there will be a good deal of prize-money from so large a ship. You, at any rate, can take things easily, my good Stine, for if anything should happen to your old man, your fate won't be very hard—you will soon have another and a younger husband. Besides, Jan Steffens always gets a double portion of any prize-money, or any treasure that is found, though all the other men risk their lives as much as he does his.'

'Oh, come now,' cried another, 'Christine has twice as much cause of anxiety as we have. We have only *one* to think of—she has *two*.'

'Two!' exclaimed Christine. 'What do you mean?'

'Why, have you not first your old husband, and then a young sweetheart in the background? I mean Kjeld Olsen.'

While Christine was reflecting what answer to make to this sudden attack, another woman said,

'There is no fear of anything happening to Kjeld Olsen to-night; he was wiser than to put himself into jeopardy, so he remained at home, and let them go without him. Of course he had good reasons for determining to spare his own life—old Jan Steffens may lose his.'

Up to this moment Christine had not made any reply to their rude jests, but her patience was now exhausted, her pale cheeks turned crimson, and rising up she said firmly,

'You have not been speaking the truth. Kjeld is to-night where he always delights to be, in the midst of danger, the boldest among the bold.'

'Who is speaking of Kjeld?' asked Skipper Ellen, who had entered the room at that moment. 'He is standing down yonder on the shore, and trying hard to persuade Poul Mikkelsen, at any price, to take him over in his boat to the English ship.'

'There now, you hear he is at home,' cried the woman, who had first mentioned the fact. 'It is well you came, Ellen, for Christine would not believe our word.'

'Will you come down to the shore?' asked Ellen; 'the rain is over, the wind has lulled, and the moon is shining clearly.'

'Yes, let us go,' said Christine, laying aside the empty coffee-cups.

'Ah! now we shall see what is the matter with poor Kjeld.'

'Of course old Jan Steffens did not care to have his company,' said the most ill-natured woman. 'No doubt he knew pretty well where Kjeld's thoughts would be wandering to.'

'And *I* say you are quite mistaken,' replied Ellen, casting a look of angry scorn on the woman. 'It would be a happy thing for you, Birthe, if you had a son, or anyone belonging to you, that resembled Kjeld.'

So saying, she took Christine by the arm and went towards the shore, followed by the rest of the women. It had ceased raining, and the wind had abated, but the sea was still much agitated, and the noise of firing was yet to be heard. Kjeld was standing in earnest conversation with an old man, who was leaning on a staff, and who shook his head occasionally as if refusing something.

'What is the matter, Kjeld?' asked Skipper Ellen. 'And why have you not gone with the rest of them?'

'Jan Steffens said there were too many in the boats,' he answered evasively.

'Ay—and now he insists upon following them,'

said the old man, 'and offers me everything he has to help him to row over yonder. But the weather is too bad. I won't trust my boat out in such a wild sea.'

'What nonsense!' cried Ellen, jeeringly. 'Are you afraid of risking your life, Poul?'

'You know better, Ellen,' replied the old man. 'I have no fear for my life, but if I lose my boat my children will starve.'

'That is a serious consideration, to be sure,' said Ellen, 'but the young man shall go, notwithstanding, and if you won't accompany him, *I* will. Come here, Kjeld—when you and I put our strength together I think we shall manage to reach the other side.'

Kjeld uttered a cry of joy, shook Ellen's hand warmly, and exclaimed, 'May God bless and reward you, dear good Ellen; I shall never forget your kindness.'

'As to your boat, Poul, you must not be alarmed if we borrow it,' said Ellen. 'If we are unlucky, and the sea takes us, my boat lies drawn up on the land, newly painted and just put to rights; and in the village yonder I have a small house—you can take both as payment if your boat be lost. But Kjeld *shall* go as he wishes.'

'Don't attempt to go, Ellen,' cried one of the women, 'you will only get into trouble.'

'With God's help I have no fear of that. The lad shall go, if we should cross in one of my fishing-boats.'

She forced herself through the circle of women who had gathered around her, and hastened to the shore, where Kjeld had already placed himself in the frail boat. Ellen got into it, and, standing up, seized an oar. Soon after the boat glided out to sea, and the somewhat hazardous voyage was begun.

'She is a wonderful woman, that Ellen!' exclaimed one of those who were looking on. 'A lucky fellow he was who got her for a wife; there's nothing she can't turn her hand to; and she can work as well as the best man among them.'

As long as it was possible to perceive the boat, it was observed to be making straight for its destination; rowed by vigorous arms, and managed by experienced persons, it seemed sometimes to be swallowed up by the waves, and then it would be seen as if riding over them, and defying them, while it never swerved from its appointed course.

'Come now, Kjeld,' cried Ellen, after they had got some distance from the land, 'let us two have a little rational conversation. It was partly to find an opportunity for this that I was so willing to go to sea with you to-night. What *really* is the matter with you, my lad? Why have you been going about latterly with your head drooping in such a melancholy way, and loitering about in idleness, instead of following your occupations cheerfully and dilligently?'

'The matter with me!' exclaimed Kjeld, in well-feigned astonishment; 'why, nothing, Ellen—you are quite mistaken in supposing that anything is the matter with me.'

'Oh, there is no use in your denying that something ails you; I am too old to be easily humbugged. You must speak the honest truth to me, Kjeld; you must be as frank with me as I am with you. You need not fear to speak freely, for no one can overhear you out thus far on the sea—no one, my boy—except myself and He who rules the ocean. You are still silent, Kjeld—then *I* will speak out. You are sighing and grieving because you love Christine Steffens, and because you think that she loves you; that's the short and the long of the matter. But have you forgotten that Christine is a married woman? and are you aware that your conduct is bringing her name into people's mouths—that every creature in the village is talking of you and her, and that the walls of her own house cannot protect her against jeering and insult? I have myself been a witness of this to-night.'

'What was said to her, Ellen?' asked Kjeld, in consternation. 'Who could speak a syllable in disparagement of Christine?'

'Say, rather, who can prevent it, Kjeld, since you yourself afford such ample room for tittle-tattle.'

'Ah, Ellen! if you only knew how much I love Christine! She has been my thought by day, and my dream by night; and when I have been away on long voyages, I denied myself everything to save all I got for her. I always expected that she would certainly one day be mine—but when I came home this autumn, she was married!'

'It was a pity. There is nothing left for you, therefore, now, but to forget her.'

'Forget her! I shall never, never forget her.'

'Oh, I have heard such vows before; young folks have always these ideas, but they smile at them when they become older. An honourable man loves a girl when he marries her, or when he intends to marry her.'

'And when he cannot marry her?'

'Then he lets her alone, my good lad, and turns his attention to some one else.'

'More easily said than done, Ellen.'

'You think I do not know what I am speaking about because I am old, and grey, and wrinkled. Is it not so, Kjeld? But remember that old people have been young themselves once, and let me tell you that the misery which you find it so impossible to bear, *I* have borne, though I am only a woman. Long ago, when I was a little better-looking than I am now, there was one who was always uppermost in my thoughts—one whom I cherished in my secret soul; in short, to whom I was as much attached as you are to Christine. He wooed me, too; he begged me to be his wife, and swore by Him who made yon heavens above that he loved only me.'

'And what answer did you give him?'

'I told him that we could not be so imprudent as to marry, for he had little, and I had still less; that I would marry the man who was the landlord of the house in which we resided, to provide a comfortable home for my mother as long as she lived. And I did marry that man. He whom I had refused never knew how much I cared for him; he did not think that I had been really attached to him. But I grieved when he went away. There never was a squall at sea that I did not think with anxiety about him; and many a night have I soaked my pillow with my tears, when I could not go to sleep because the tempest raged so without.'

'Do I know the person of whom you are speaking, Ellen?'

'Yes, you do, Kjeld: he is your own father.'

'My father!'

'Can you now comprehend why I have always taken such an interest in you, and why I have some right to advise you to let Christine alone? I do not say that you must forget her.'

'No, because you are convinced it is impossible for me to do so.'

'Not at all—because I know forgetfulness will come of itself. I only desire to impress on you the necessity of leaving this place, and no longer loitering about the sea-shore here. To-morrow I am going to sail to Æro, or Æbler, and if you will come with me, Kjeld, we will go on to Copenhagen. You had better engage yourself on board some ship going to the south, and stay away a few years. When you come back again, if our Lord has spared my life till then, you will thank me for the advice I have given you this night. But see! here are our boats. For God's sake, Kjeld, do your duty! I will fasten our little skiff to one of the gunboats.'

Christine in the meantime remained standing on the beach at a little distance from the other women. She had been a silent but much interested spectator of all that had occurred previous to Kjeld's and Ellen's departure, and she stood watching the frail little boat as long as it was visible. At length the fisherwomen rejoined her, and were loud in the expression of their fears and forebodings. Christine said scarcely anything.

'Of course you have no reason to be afraid, Christine,' said the same woman who had before commenced jeering at her in Jan Steffens's house.

'Kjeld cannot arrive yonder until all the dangerous work is over, but he can always boast of being one of the party, and perhaps he may get a share of the prize-money. And if any accident should happen to old Jan Steffens, you will have a new protector ready at hand.'

'What do you mean by all the insinuations you have been throwing out to-night?' asked Christine.

'Well, this is too good!' cried the woman,

laughing, and turning towards the other females. 'She pretends to be so ignorant, the little lamb!'

'But speak out—explain yourself! I do not understand a word you have been saying, and cannot imagine what you have been all driving at to-night.'

'I mean that you and Kjeld will marry as soon as Jan's eyes are closed for ever, and that it is no fault of yours or Kjeld's that this has been so long of taking place.'

'And will you listen to my answer?' said Christine, in a peremptory tone, and speaking with such pointed distinctness that her words were perfectly heard by every one near. 'If such a misfortune should befall me that any accident shall occur to Jan Steffens to-night, I swear that I will never marry either Kjeld Olsen, or any other man upon this earth.'

'Oh, you would think better of it—you would change your mind,' cried the other, laughing scornfully.

'No!' said Christine. 'By my hopes of salvation and eternal happiness in the world to come, I speak the truth. And I beseech you to believe me, and leave me in peace.'

Shortly after the firing ceased, and many eyes

were turned anxiously towards the place where it was known the ship lay.

'It is over now,' said a solemn voice. 'They will be coming back presently. God have mercy on us all, but especially on those who have lost any near and dear to them!'

There was a deep and unbroken silence among the crowd. Terror and anxiety had closed all their lips, and every eye was strained looking out for the boats. Old Poul Mikkelsen, who had clambered up to the top of a pile of rocks, was sitting without his hat, and singing the first verses of a psalm in a weak and tremulous voice. Suddenly there burst forth a bright light in the direction of the ship; it increased in width until by degrees it became a broad sheet of dark flame, the glowing reflection of which streamed over the waves and tinged the hills that skirted the adjacent coast. Such was the glare of light that the shore at Fyensland could be seen crowded with people, and several boats were discerned apparently rowing in great haste to and from the corvette.

'The ship is on fire!' cried Poul. 'Our people have been victorious.'

The fire seemed to increase until at length it

appeared to become concentrated, when it shot up in one high pillar of flame, from which jets of sparks were thrown up into the air around. While the group on the shore at Lyngspoint were standing in breathless silence, the church clock at Erizö was heard to strike three, and the grey dawn of morning began to give place to the clear light of day. In the glare from the fire the corvette—with its slender masts, its yards, and cordage—became distinctly and fearfully visible, and people could be perceived hurrying up and down the deck. Shortly after, the guns went off, the fire having then reached them, and one cannon-ball struck the bank at no great distance from where the wives and families of the fishermen were assembled. No one seemed to notice it, for the thoughts of all were earnestly bent upon the terrible drama which was being enacted out upon the sea; each person present had a deep interest in it, and not one of them but waited for its *dénoûment* with dread and apprehension.

'Here come our boats!' cried Poul, pointing with his staff towards two dark specks which were to be seen tossing on the waves at a little distance from the corvette. Soon after a third boat was observed, towed by one of the gun-boats. Christine had been the first to perceive it; she folded her hands, and cast a grateful look of thanksgiving up towards heaven.

At length the gunboats reached the shore. In the deeply-affecting scene that followed were mingled joyous exclamations and groans of despair—smiles and tears—as those so dear and so anxiously looked for were found to be safe, or, alas! to be among the wounded and the dead. Christine's eyes sought Jan everywhere—but in vain—she did not see him. She covered her face, and burst into tears.

In a few minutes Kjeld approached her, and laid his hand gently on her arm.

'Where is my husband?' she asked, impatiently.

'He is dead,' replied Kjeld.

'Dead! dead!' exclaimed Christine, in a voice faint and trembling from agitation.

'Yes! He fell at the very moment that he ordered us to return to our boats, when the Englishmen had set fire to the corvette. I did all I could to save him, dear Christine; I posted myself at his side, and defended him to the last. But it was all in vain; it was impossible to rescue him from death.'

'Why did you not go with him at first?' asked Christine abruptly.

'Because he insisted that I should not. He knew all that we, too, have felt and thought; he desired me to remain behind, and carry a message to you, but I was not to deliver it until to-morrow.'

'It will be needless,' said Christine. 'To-morrow I shall be gone to my aunt at Kjærup.'

She stretched out both her hands to him, and struggling with her tears, she added, in a tone of deep emotion.

'God be with you, Kjeld! my dear, my only friend!'

'You are not going away, Christine?' exclaimed Kjeld.

'Yes,' she replied. 'I made a vow to the Almighty that I would do so when I offered up my prayers to Him to bring you back unhurt.'

'But still why must you go away?' he asked, in a voice of alarm and anxiety.

'Because we two must forget our hopes and our dreams; because we must separate from each other, never more to meet again!'

AUNT FRANCISCA.

FROM THE DANISH OF CARL BERNHARD.

CHAPTER I.

On a lovely summer evening, in the month of July, an old lady was to be seen walking alone by the row of small houses which forms one side of St. Anne's Place, and stretches down towards the harbour. This part of Copenhagen contains the domiciles of the fashionable world; it is what the Faubourg Saint-Germain used to be to the Parisians; palace succeeds to palace, the Court is situated in this neighbourhood, and the foreign diplomatists—a class more important in Copenhagen than perhaps in any other place on earth—honour this portion of the city by making it their abode. But, as it were, to remind the world that great people cannot do without the poorer sort, certain small houses have here and there thrust themselves into good society, and the many signboards hanging out plainly evince that their inhabitants do not wear laurels so easily won, or enjoy such luxurious repose as their neighbours do. At any rate, such certainly is the case with the dwellers in the row of houses above mentioned, which, from one end to the other, is occupied by mechanics, seafaring men, and other common people.

The old lady walked so slowly that you could easily perceive she was already on the shady side of life; her carriage was stiff, and her steps measured, as if she moved with some difficulty; yet it was evident that she had some determined object earnestly in view. Her features were sharp, and denoted firmness; indeed, they might have been thought harsh and forbidding, had not her mild blue eyes imparted an expression of tenderness and goodness to her otherwise stern countenance. I know not if my description is clear enough to convey to my readers any idea of the face that now stands before my mind's eye, but Aunt Francisca's countenance was always somewhat of a difficult problem, and this must be my excuse if I have failed in the delineation of it. Her dress was in keeping with her general appearance; it was in the fashion of a bygone period, at least twenty years old in make and materials, and yet one might in vain have sought for a single spot or crease in it. There were such fastidious cleanliness, and such a degree of scrupulous neatness visible over her whole person, that the beholder at once felt assured an old maid was before him. Be this said without any disrespect to other ladies, whose *nicety* I am far from calling in question.

With an extensive parasol in her hand, and a large and apparently heavy silken bag over her arm, the old lady advanced towards a house whose exterior denoted that it was occupied by people belonging to the lower classes. She did not scan the number of the houses, and her feet seemed mechanically to have found its threshold, as if she had often passed over it. And so she had, in truth. A young woman, with a child in her arms, opened the door to her, and exclaimed,

'Is it really you, my dear lady? Our Lord himself must send you here to us, poor miserable creatures!'

The speaker and the infant she held in her arms were both clad in absolute tatters. The child looked like a monster in a magic glass, shrivelled up, yellow skinned, with sunken but staring eyes, and wrinkled, though scarcely yet two years of age. It would have been difficult to have determined which bore the palm for dirt and disorder, the room or its inhabitants.

The elderly lady looked about in vain for a place where she might seat herself.

'You do not deserve that I should come more frequently to visit you,' the lady said; 'all hope of assisting you is at an end when you yourself will do nothing to improve your condition. In what state is this that I find you? You promised me that when next I came I should see everything tidy about you.'

The woman cast down her eyes at this reproachful greeting, and remained silent. She placed the child on the floor while she dusted with the shreds of an old garment a wooden stool, the only seat in the room. The lady looked compassionately at the child, and said, in a less stern voice,

'What you will not do for your own comfort's sake, you will surely not refuse to do for the sake of your poor children. The unfortunate little creatures will perish amidst all this dirt; it *must* engender disease. Where are the other children? Has the eldest gone to school yet?'

The poor woman looked much embarrassed, and

stammered a few words which it was impossible to comprehend. The lady continued her interrogations :

'And your husband—has he got any work? Why did he never go to the place where I told him he could obtain employment? Because he prefers remaining in idleness to attempting any useful occupation—he would rather spend in rioting the few pence he can scrape together, than work to place himself beyond want and wretchedness. What will be the end of these courses?'

'Ah, my good lady, you are quite right,' replied the woman; 'my husband, the good-for-nothing that he is, is the cause of all our misery. He will not let spirits alone, and every penny we have goes down his throat in strong drink. I beg pardon for mentioning this to you, madam, who no doubt have a fine, good gentleman for a husband, but men-folks in *our* rank are dreadful creatures; I often wish I had never married.'

'Very likely your husband has the same improper feeling towards you, and upon as good grounds,' replied the old lady. 'Married people should bear with each other, and share their burdens between them as well as their pleasures. A disorderly wife has no right to complain of a disorderly husband. It is a woman's duty to make home comfortable; *that* can be done at little cost, but it cannot be done without order and cleanliness. All that I have seen here proves that you are quite as much in fault as your husband. Where is the yarn for which I gave you money? Have you bought the flax?'

The poor woman burst into tears, and began to protest that she was not to blame. Had she known the lady's name, or where she resided, she would have come to her in her trouble. But she was ignorant of both; the landlord had threatened to turn them out into the street if they did not pay their rent; and she had nothing to give him, no means of keeping a roof over their heads except by handing him the money entrusted to her, which she was assured by her husband there was no sin in disposing of in this way, as it had been a gift. The old lady inquired more minutely into the state of their affairs, remonstrated with the young woman, scolded her, and threatened to withdraw the assistance she gave them if they would not make some exertion for the future to help themselves, and finished by drawing forth from the large silk bag sundry articles of food and clothing, which she laid on the table before the unfortunate mother. She then took the infant up from the floor, kissed it, and gave it some nice wheaten bread and a new dress, and promised the mother that she would give the child an entire suit of new clothes if, on her next visit, she found everything clean and in order. Bestowing upon her once more some earnest injunctions, the lady left the house without waiting to listen to the poor woman's thanks and blessings.

When she went up the street it was with the same measured steps, and the same prim air as before; the large silk bag hung from her left arm, but it was empty now, while she held daintily with two fingers of her right hand the old-fashioned parasol. Thus she walked on until she reached a house in Bredegade, where resided a relation of hers named Werner, the widow of a councillor of state,* who had two daughters, of whom the elder was called Louise, the younger Flora. Louise was a very quiet girl and of a retiring disposition; she was betrothed and soon to be married to Rudolph Horn, a young lawyer, who had a great deal of business, and was possessed of a good private

* Councillor of state. Etatsraad is a Danish title, and an etatsraad's wife is styled Etatsraadinde.

fortune besides. Flora was secretly engaged to Lieutenant Arnold—secretly, that is to say, the engagement had not been declared, though everybody was aware of it. It might be a tolerable match when he became a captain, but it would probably be a dozen years or more before he obtained his company. They were both young, however, and time flies rapidly, as everybody knows, so they consoled themselves with hope.

The family were sitting in an arbour in the garden, as they often did in summer; Arnold had brought a new novel which he had just commenced reading aloud to them. The ladies—their number increased by the addition of two cousins, who frequently visited them—sat round the table with their work, exceedingly interested in the novel, which began 'so charmingly,' and promised to be 'so interesting,' when Arnold happened to look up, and glancing along the garden-walk, exclaimed,

'May I be shot, if stalking towards us yonder is not—yes, it is herself! I have the honour to announce Aunt Francisca's august arrival.'

The girls all cast looks of annoyance at the old lady, who was slowly approaching the arbour where they were assembled. 'How very tiresome!' exclaimed the little party as with one voice, while Arnold threw his book angrily on the table, and said,

'Now we must give up knowing the rest of this new story, for I have to return the volume to its owner early to-morrow morning. What unlucky chance can have brought that wearisome old spectre here this evening, I wonder?'

Louise rose and went to meet the old lady. Aunt Francisca curtseyed, and then kissed her on both cheeks. Mrs. Werner and Flora underwent the same species of greeting. A heavy, forced conversation was then carried on about the weather and the pleasure of having a garden in Copenhagen. Arnold took no part in it, although Aunt Francisca frequently addressed herself to him; Mrs. Werner was the only one who maintained it with decent civility, for people advanced in years can bear disappointments better than young persons.

'Will Rudolph soon return from Holstein?' asked the old lady of Louise; 'it is surprising that he has not written to me. You can tell him, my dear, that I have been expecting a letter from him on both the last post-days.'

'That is devilish cool! A nice piece of pretension on the part of such an antiquated virago,' observed Arnold, in a half-whisper.

Cousin Ida could not refrain from giggling.

'You seem to be quite in a laughing humour, my child,' said Miss Francisca.

'Have you been to the German plays yet?' asked Flora of the old lady, with a furtive smile to the rest of the party.

'No, my head can't stand theatres now,' replied Aunt Francisca. 'They do not suit my age, and, indeed, I see so badly that I could not enjoy acting. Have you been there?'

Mrs. Werner answered her, and plunged into a disquisition on some of the plays, and on the parts of the performers, but Aunt Francisca heard them without any apparent interest. She afterwards entered on the subject of the Bible Society and its great usefulness, but was listened to in return with apathy and suppressed yawns; nobody *there* cared about Bible societies. Flora proposed that they should drink tea a little earlier than usual, and Louise went to order it. The conversation came to a dead stand; at length Aunt Francisca said, 'I am afraid my visit is inconvenient to you this evening; you might have been going out—perhaps to the German play?'

'We were only going to have read aloud a book which I brought with me,' said Arnold. 'There is no German play to-night; but they are performing at Price's, and if the ladies are inclined to go, we shall be quite in time.'

'So speaks youth — distances are nothing for them,' said the old lady, with a smile, under which she attempted to hide the unpleasant feeling she experienced at finding herself unwelcome. 'You must not mind me, my dear cousins; I should be sorry to put you to any inconvenience, and am going presently.'

But Mrs. Werner begged her to stay, assuring her that the tale could be read some other time, and that nobody had dreamed of going to Price's; Arnold was only joking.

'That other time must be during the night, then.' said Arnold, in no very dulcet tone, 'for I have promised to return the book to-morrow morning, without fail.'

Aunt Francisca did not hear his civil speech, for she was talking to Mrs. Werner. The young people put their heads together, and whispered to each other. Judging by their glances, it was evident that the old maiden visitor was the subject of their remarks. One criticized her arms, another her bonnet, a third her parasol.

'But what do you say to that huge foraging-sack hanging from her arm? Can any one inform me for what she carries it?' said Arnold. 'It would hold at least half a bushel of corn. Perhaps the stingy old animal goes to the market to buy all her own provisions, for fear that her servant-girl should make a penny or two out of them now and then.'

'Nonsense; she is too prim to venture among the market folks,' said Ida. 'But she fancies it is fashionable. Dare you attack her about it, Flora?'

Flora wished to show her courage, but could scarcely speak for laughing, as she took up Aunt Francisca's bag, and said,

'This is a very pretty bag; the embroidery is à la Grecque, is it not?'

Miss Francisca replied gravely, '*Pretty?* You cannot possibly mean that, my child; it is as ugly as a bag can be, but it holds a good deal, and therefore I use it sometimes. Living so much alone as I do, I must occasionally go my own errands.'

Flora looked foolish, and stammered a few words in defence of the bag, while she coloured deeply;

but the old lady pretended not to observe her embarrassment, and she continued: 'I think it *really* very pretty, but it should not be seen near this lovely shawl, which certainly puts it to shame.' So saying, she took up a little muslin shawl, beautifully embroidered in gold and coloured flowers, which was lying on the table.

'I am glad you admire it, my dear,' said the old lady, 'for I have often intended to beg your acceptance of it. I have another at home exactly like it, which I intend for Louise; they are too gay for my time of life.'

Flora was much pleased with the gift, and had just thanked her cousin—for the old lady, though generally called among her young connections 'Aunt Francisca,' was by no means so nearly related to them—when Ida whispered, 'Why, it is real East Indian! Well, it was lucky for you that I persuaded you to go into raptures about the hideous bag—set to now and praise her high-heeled shoes. Who knows what they may yield?'

'Shame on you, Ida. Do you think I am going to be rude to her again?' said Flora.

Aunt Francisca found the evening air rather chilly, and hinted that it would be as well to repair to the more comfortable drawing-room within doors. Many were the glances of anger and annoyance which passed among the young people when Mrs. Werner thereupon desired the servant to carry the tea-things back to the house, and they had all to rise in order to leave the garden. Arnold, of course, gallantly assisted the young ladies in putting up their work and carrying their work-boxes, while he exercised his witty propensities at the expense of Miss Francisca. Flora meanwhile offered her arm to the old lady, who, however, did not proceed immediately to the house, but expressed a wish to look first at some of the flower-beds.

When they were alone, she turned suddenly towards Flora, and said,

'Tell me, my dear girl, are you engaged to Lieutenant Arnold? Perhaps you will think that it is no business of mine whether you are or not; but whatever is of consequence to you is interesting to me, and it is not from mere curiosity that I ask you. Ah! I saw how he pressed your hand. . . . Come, you must not deny it, for I saw it distinctly. Though I am old, I have sharper eyes and ears than people may fancy. But you know, my dear, girls should not allow gentlemen to squeeze their hands unless they are actually engaged to them. It would be quite improper otherwise.'

Flora cast down her eyes, but made no reply.

'I know that you are a very good, sensible girl, and that is why I like you so much; but truth must be told and listened to, although it is not always palatable. What are the prospects now-a-days of a lieutenant in the army? Poor indeed, my child; it would be almost an eternity before you could marry. In the meantime there might be a hundred flirtations, and the first love might be left in the lurch. Arnold is very flighty, and I fear also very imprudent. I know that he is in debt, and that leads to beggary.'

'But all young men get into debt, Aunt Francisca,' replied Flora, in a low, subdued voice.

'Bless you, child! how can you say so? Correct and respectable persons do *not* run into debt. Rudolph does not owe a shilling to anyone—I could take my oath to that.'

'But there is no necessity for Rudolph to fall into debt. Seeing that he has a good private fortune, he has no great merit in keeping out of it. But what can a poor young officer do who has nothing but his pay to live on?'

'He has no business by his flattery and fair words to entice a girl into an engagement which he cannot carry out,' said Miss Francisca; 'that is altogether indefensible. The age of miracles is past; no bird will come flying into your window with gold on its bill, and in our days people don't live on air. Do you really imagine that love is so durable a feeling that it can withstand adversity, privations, and time itself, which conquers all things? Love and inconstancy are half-sisters, dear Flora. Ten years hence you will be called an old maid, though, if married, you would be still considered at that age a young woman. In twenty years from this time it would be positively ridiculous on your part to think of marrying, yet Arnold could scarcely venture to take a wife before then.'

Flora played with her sash, and her eyes filled with tears, whilst the gloom that overspread her countenance showed how disagreeable the conversation was to her. Aunt Francisca looked earnestly at her, and putting her arm gently round her waist, asked, in a low voice,

'Are you betrothed to Arnold, my child? Answer me truly, Flora—are you or are you not?'

The girl tried to speak, but her lips closed again.

She looked at the pretty East India handkerchief, and in her embarrassment crushed it between her fingers. The old lady withdrew her arm, and stooped to pick a flower.

'Come, my dear,' she said, 'let us go in; it is getting quite chill, and the evening air is not for old people like me. Your roses are beautiful; permit me to take one or two home for my flower-vase.'

Flora hastened to gather a bouquet of flowers, and then accompanied Miss Francisca to the house, the latter talking on indifferent subjects.

'What did she want with you?' asked one of the cousins. 'Did she give you anything besides the little shawl?'

'Oh, I wish she had kept her shawl,' said Flora, sharply. 'When presents have to be paid for by listening to stupid prosy lectures, I, for one, would rather dispense with the gifts. She is a tiresome old maid as ever lived.'

Louise was presiding at the tea-table, so Aunt Francisca sat down near her, and did not again approach Flora, who seemed out of spirits, and spoke neither to the old lady nor to Arnold. When the latter attempted to whisper something to her, she drew back pointedly without listening to him, and with a toss of her head which plainly showed Arnold that she was out of humour. Arnold looked at Miss Francisca as if he could have murdered her, and muttered: 'This is that old wretch's fault, I'll be bound. A starched old maid like her would infect a whole regiment of young girls with her prudery. I suppose I shall be expected to see that ancient piece of goods home—and if I am compelled to undertake this pleasing office, she shall come to grief, for I swear I will contrive to make her fall and break one of her old legs.'

If Louise had not spoken from time to time, not a word would have been uttered the whole evening; she was the only one who took any trouble to keep up a little conversation. Arnold placed himself by the window, and drummed listlessly with his fingers on the panes of glass: Flora sewed diligently, as if her daily bread depended on her getting through a certain quantity of work. Madame Werner knitted with equal perseverance, and only occasionally contributed a 'yes' or a 'no' to the conversation; the cousins cast sidelong glances towards Arnold, and tittered. At length nine o'clock struck, and it was announced that Miss Francisca's servant had come for her. Everybody seemed relieved — and the old lady rose instantly, as if she felt that her company was unwelcome, and that the sooner she took her departure the better. Madame Werner squeezed out an invitation for her to stay a little longer, but it was not accepted.

When Arnold found that she was really going, he strode up to her, and asked if he might have the pleasure of escorting her home; at which request the cousins could not restrain their laughter, and Flora had to bite her lips to prevent herself from following their example, while Louise did her utmost to prevent the old lady from observing the rudeness of her relations. Her back was scarcely turned before every tongue in the drawing-room she had just quitted became loosened, and the sounds of mirth and laughter could be distinctly heard by her before she had even left the house. When Louise, who had quitted the room with Aunt Francisca, to see her well wrapped up, returned to it, she attacked them for their rudeness in laughing, and talking so loud as soon as she had left the room, when they had been sitting in solemn silence the whole evening previously. Madame Werner sided with Louise, but Arnold was not to be checked in his rejoicings at having got rid of the stupid, tiresome old maid.

Poor Miss Francisca, meanwhile, heard the shouts of laughter as she walked up the street, and looking up sadly at the windows she thought: 'They are rejoicing at my departure; even there I am *de trop*.' But on her servant remarking how uncommonly gay they were at Madame Werner's, she only replied, 'They are a very lively, happy family, and long may they remain so.'

When the 'happy family' were relieved of her presence, the novel reading was resumed—and it was late before the tale was finished, and the party separated. After the young ladies had retired to the room which they shared together, Flora exclaimed, as she put away the pretty Indian shawl, ' Aunt Francisca is a very good soul, but she is abominably tiresome—it is hardly possible to put up with her.'

'I should think that where there is much real worth, a little peculiarity of manner might easily be borne with,' replied Louise; but Flora laughed as she said,

'Nothing is so bad as to be wearisome dear Louise; I can't endure anyone who bores me.'

Six weeks had elapsed since Miss Francisca's visit above recorded; autumn was approaching, the evenings were becoming longer, and the leaves of the trees assuming a yellow tint. It was on a grey afternoon in September that a young man passed slowly along Halmtorv, in Copenhagen, and stopped before a small house which looked as if it were the abode of death, for the blinds were all down, although there were no lights inside. The street-door was locked, and it was not till long after he had rung that it was opened by an elderly woman, who had on a black dress and black ribbons in her cap. They recognized each other gravely and then the young man, who seemed familiar with the house, ascended the stairs, and entered a room on the first floor, whilst the servant carefully locked the outer door. The apartment which he entered was empty, not an article of furniture relieved the bareness of the walls, and before the windows hung long white curtains, closely drawn; in the centre of the room there was a square space, where the uncovered boards looked white and shining, but the rest of the floor was thickly strewed with fine sand, and on that again lay flowers and green leaves taken from trees, which in the four corners of the room were formed into elaborate patterns.

The young man stopped on the threshold of the floor, and gazed sadly at the empty desolation before him. He was speedily joined by the old servant, who placed herself by his side, and also contemplated sorrowfully the square space, as if she recalled in thought what had so lately occupied it. Then, turning her eyes towards the young man, and perceiving by the expression of his countenance what was passing in his mind, she held out her hand to him in silence, which he took and pressed warmly. She was a trustworthy, affectionate creature, a servant of the olden time, such as are scarcely ever to be met with now in families of our modern days.

Presently the young man crossed the room, stepping lightly, as if he were afraid to crush the already fading flowers, and opened the door to another apartment, where, as in the first, long white curtains, drawn across the half-closed windows, gave a dim sad tone to the tasteful furniture and gay-coloured carpet. He was followed by the old servant, who told him that he would find the keys belonging to her late mistress in her own little daily sitting-room, and that all her keeping places were in perfect order. 'Alas! sir,' she added, 'how miserable it is for me to be left behind. I had always hoped and prayed that our Lord would graciously call me first.'

'It is the course of nature in this world, Inger,' he replied, 'that the eldest should go first. Your mistress was almost ten years older than you.'

'Very true, sir. Had my dear mistress lived till next Candlemas, she would have completed her sixty-seventh year, and I shall be fifty-seven come next March. Three-and-twenty years have I lived with her, and I can testify to her goodness in every respect; she was such a benefactress to the poor. Oh! how many of them will miss her!'

And Inger began to weep bitterly; her tears were of genuine sorrow for the loss of her kind mistress, for Rodolph, who was the nearest of kin to the deceased lady, had already told the faithful servant that a comfortable provision should be made for her, so as to secure to her independence for the rest of her life.

Rudolph Horn was the legal heir of Miss Francisca Garlov, who had that day been buried. She had been his mother's first cousin and dearest friend, they had been almost brought up together, and their intimacy had subsisted without any diminution, until death had separated them, thirteen years before, by removing Rudolph's mother from this world. The old maid had transferred the friendship for the mother to the son ; when he came to Copenhagen, as a student, her house had always been open to him, and she gave him to understand that he should inherit whatever she might leave. She had died after a very few days' illness, and Rudolph, who was at the time in the country, though he hastened to Copenhagen the moment he heard of her mere indisposition, had not arrived in time to see his old friend alive.

As he sat in her now deserted parlour, his memory retraced the days of his childhood, when he used to visit her along with his mother, and when he used to admire the Chinese pagodas and mandarins which ornamented her sitting-room, her old china teacups, her pretty inlaid tea-table, her large well-stuffed easy-chair, her chiffoniers with mirrors and gilding in the doors, and, above all, a certain japanned cabinet, that had always to be opened to let 'the dear boy' see the pretty things in it, and some one or other of which was generally bestowed on him, for 'Aunt Francisca' never let him go empty-handed from her house. Ah! how different were the desires which filled his soul *then* and *now;* a whole lifetime almost seemed to lie between these two periods of his existence; he was then only eight years old, and now he was thirty!

Old Inger brought in candles, and offered to go through an inventory of the furniture and effects with him, but Rudolph told her that was quite unnecessary, as he had entire confidence in her; however, he took the key of Miss Francisca's bureau, as Inger informed him that it was the last injunction of her beloved mistress that he should be requested to open that depository of her papers immediately after her funeral.

Rudolph looked at his watch, as if he would fain have found that it was too late that evening to examine the papers of the deceased; but it was only six o'clock, and he had no excuse for putting off his painful task. It was some little time, however, after he had opened the bureau, before he could bring himself to disturb the neat packets of letters, and other little articles, arranged with so much order in this depository of the good old lady's treasures. He felt that it was almost a sin to touch these relics of the past, and merely half-opened the various drawers, more to obey the wishes of the dead than to search into their contents; but when he came to a hidden compartment, and unlocked its little door, he beheld what riveted his attention, for in it were two miniatures, a few papers, and two or three manuscript books. One of the miniatures was the likeness of a very handsome young man, dressed according to the fashion of a bygone period. The complexion was florid, rather than pale; the dark blue eyes expressed at once thoughtfulness and mirth, and round the mouth played a gay smile, while the smooth forehead gave no evidence of care or sorrow; the cravat was carelessly tied, imparting an idea of negligence in attire, which contrasted rather oddly with the elaborate ruffles that appeared below the brown coat sleeves, and coquettishly shaded a hand of delicate whiteness.

Close to this miniature lay another, which evidently portrayed 'Aunt Francisca' in her earlier years. She was pale, but with pretty features, finely-arched eyebrows, and a face altogether pleasing, from its expression of goodness and cheerfulness. Her hair, which fell in rich curls over her slender throat, was confined by a light-blue ribbon, and her dress had the peaked stomacher worn in those days.

Here, then, was a clue to the history of Aunt Francisca's youth; after so many silent years, these portraits, hidden away together, told a tale of the past—a tale, doubtless, of sorrow and disappointment. How little do the friends and acquaintances, made in after-life, know of the feelings, the hopes, the dreams, and the incidents of earlier years, many of which are hushed into deep mystery until the grave has received its prey, when some cherished token, some treasured reminiscence may unfold the secrets of days gone by.

When Rudolph had gazed for a time on these interesting faces, he replaced the miniatures where he had found them, and proceeded to examine the papers. Among them were memoranda and account-books, which showed how well regulated the affairs of the deceased had been, and how her economy had afforded her ample means to do good to those around her. He continued to read the documents before him until he became quite absorbed in them; and he was sitting at the old bureau, forgetful of the flight of time, until the clock struck nine. Its unwearied tongue, which amidst life and death ceased not to give forth its warning tones, aroused him from his dreamy mood, and, snatching one more glance at Aunt Francisca's likeness, he closed the bureau, and calling Inger, he prepared to depart. The old woman lighted him to the door, and attempted to draw him into conversation, but he shook his head and hurried out, with tears in his eyes.

'Ah!' said Inger, to herself, as she returned to her solitary chamber, 'how kind-hearted Herr Rudolph is—so different from most young men now-a-days, who are ashamed to let people see that they have any feelings at all!'

CHAPTER II.

On leaving the abode so recently visited by death, Rudolph repaired to a house in Bredgade, where, as he was ringing at the door, he heard, even in the street, the sound of laughter in the drawing-room above. Annoyed at this, he drew back a few steps, and, observing lights blazing through the windows, he shrank from encountering the gaiety within, and was about to go away, but when the door was opened, he changed his mind, and slowly ascended the stairs.

Whilst he had been sitting in Aunt Francisca's deserted parlour, a gay little party had been gathering around Mrs. Werner's tea-table. They were all young, with the exception of the lady of the house. Flora was making tea, and Lieutenant Arnold was by her side, rendering her what assistance he could. Mrs. Werner sat near them, more to sanction the attention Arnold was paying the pretty Flora, than to check it. Louise was at the opposite side of the table, with some fancy-work in her hand, taking little or no part in the gossiping that was going on, but glancing from time to time anxiously at the timepiece in the room, as its hands pointed to half-past eight, a quarter to nine, nine o'clock, a quarter past nine, and Rudolph had not made his appearance.

The two cousins, who were mentioned on a former occasion—young ladies—and two or three young men, relations also of the family, made up the party. Mrs. Werner and her daughters were in slight mourning, in consequence of the death of Miss Francisca, but the gaiety which was going on gave no evidence of sorrow for her loss. The smiling countenances, the well-lighted room, the open pianoforte, with some fashionable waltzes on the stand, all formed a strong contrast to the scene Rudolph had just quitted, and he almost frowned as he entered the room.

Louise arose and went forward to meet him, while Flora laughingly scolded him for being so late.

'I beg a thousand pardons,' said Rudolph, 'but it was impossible for me to come earlier.'

'Mercy on us, what a tragical face! You look as if you were bound to follow Aunt Francisca into the very grave itself. There, console yourself with a cup of cold tea; it is your own fault that it is not better. Don't pet him so, Louise. Do you not see how melancholy he is?'

'Melancholy people are just those who need to be petted,' said Louise, moving her chair so as to make room for him by her; 'others don't require it.'

'It is really quite touching to see the deeply-distressed heir of Aunt Francisca's china pagodas, putting on the solemn look of an undertaker, on account of her, alas! too early departure from this world,' said Flora. 'Most faithful of swains, where will you find such another interesting shepherdess of sixty-seven years of age?'

'What, is it possible,' cried one of the young men, 'that Rudolph is grieving for old Miss Garlov? It seems to me that the best thing the ancient skin-flint could do was to lay herself down and die. Heaven knows there are plenty of old maids left in the world!'

'She was a worthy creature—a good soul,' said Mrs. Werner, with perfect indifference, 'and, doubtless, is now happy in the other world. There is no need to lament those who go to a better life; they are well off.'

'She will be wafted, like an airy being, up to the highest heaven, on account of her unimpeachable virtue,' said Arnold, laughing at his own wit. Rudolph looked angrily at him, and was about to say something, when Louise laid her hand on his arm to stop him. There was an awkward silence for a few minutes, until one of the cousins exclaimed:

'I wonder if Miss Francisca ever had a lover.'

'I should think not,' replied Mrs. Werner, with a half smile. 'She did not look like a person who would have admirers.'

'Admirers!' cried one of the young men. 'Fancy anybody making love to such a prude. I don't suppose she ever had the most distant idea of love.'

'One can have very good fun with old maids, sometimes,' said Arnold; 'one can quiz them about their youthful conquests, or persuade them that Peter or Paul is casting, even now, sheeps' eyes at them; but it would have been impossible to have brought Miss Garlov into this state of happy delusion; there was no tampering with *her*.'

'What a tiresome person she was!' exclaimed cousin Ida. 'A terrible bore!'

'Heavens! yes! Such an old maid as she was is positively a horror, enough to scare one,' said Arnold, 'though I don't call myself faint-hearted, and am certainly not apt to flee from the fair sex. But these wrinkled, pinched-up pieces of propriety, who are always denouncing the immorality and folly of youth, don't deserve to be included under the head of "fair." Well, had I known that Aunt Francisca was to be buried to-day, I certainly should have followed her to the grave, out of gratitude to her for taking this last journey, never more to return.'

'My cousin did not trouble you much, I think,' said Rudolph, angrily. 'She came here but seldom, and was never fond of annoying people.'

Arnold made some ill-natured answer, continuing to quiz poor Miss Francisca. Everyone laughed except Louise, who was anxiously watching Rudolph's countenance, and much afraid lest he should make some severe remark.

Flora, enjoying the scene, said: 'See how Louise is labouring to keep Rudolph quiet, for he is quite ready to do battle with us all. Ever since I have known him, he has been the faithful knight of all forlorn old maids.'

'And all young ladies should, therefore, feel gratitude to me,' said Rudolph, ' for not one of them—I make no exceptions—can declare, with certainty, that she may not one day or other become an old maid.'

Flora cast a glance towards Arnold, which plainly said that she, at least, had nothing to do with the threatened calamity.

Rudolph continued: 'I have often observed with surprise how youth, especially early youth, hates and despises old maids. Why is it that age, which demands respect for all others, should, in civilized society, exclude unmarried ladies from it? I do not allude to my deceased relative in particular, nor will I dwell on all her kindness to me—I will only speak of her as one of a class, one among the many who share her fate. We were all acquainted with her, and therefore I ask you, who have just been casting ridicule on her memory, if you have *really* felt the bitter contempt you have expressed for her? I think I can answer for you, No. Not one of you is, in point of fact, so bad-hearted as you would make yourselves appear by your thoughtless chattering.' Rudolph looked earnestly round, but not one present attempted to reply.

He went on: 'Is an old maid's lot so delightful, that people must try to annoy her by scorn? *I* should say not. Should we not rather be sorry to see anyone excluded from what many of us value most? A life without interest, or close domestic ties, is not to be envied; nor is it the fault of the woman if she is not destined to become a wife and a mother. Many single women have but to look back in their advancing years on a wasted life; to remember names that no more must be uttered by them; to feel the void in their hearts to which no amount of resignation can make them insensible; and to all this must be added an endless struggle against those who have been more fortunate than themselves, and enforced patience with the jeers and scoffs launched so pitilessly against them. How few girls look forward to this position for their after-years! And yet circumstances not calculated upon, the factitious wants entailed on us by society, the poverty which forbids many a union, the fickle fancies of men, or an evil destiny, which seems sometimes to delight in thwarting the dearest hopes, and sundering those who might have been happy together, may doom them to it. And is all this only a subject for ridicule? For my part, I cannot laugh at an old maid, even if she loves only her cat or her canary-bird. God has implanted affections in her heart; mankind have rejected these, therefore she loves animals of a lower species, who seem grateful for her kindness. Ludwig said, a few minutes ago, that Aunt Francisca looked as if she had never had a lover. Could that be possible, with her mild eyes, her sweet face, her amiable disposition? She had more goodness in her little finger than most people have in their whole person; but none of you knew her well!'

'Nonsense, Rudolph!' exclaimed Mrs. Werner. 'How can you pretend to say we did not know her? I am sure *I* have been acquainted with her for at least a score of years; she was a second cousin of my lamented husband.'

'Nevertheless, I maintain that none of you *did* know her well. If not disagreeable to you, I should like to tell you Aunt Francisca's history as I have heard it from my mother, who was her most intimate friend, and partly from herself. I have also found out much from her private papers, which, by her own wish, I looked over this very evening. Now that she is gone, the story of her life need no longer be a secret.'

'Hark ye, Rudolph,' said Mrs. Werner, stretching across, and whispering to him. 'In regard to *that* secret, I would rather you did not touch upon it'; her imprudence in early life, which caused so much annoyance to her family, had better not be related in the presence of young girls like my daughters and their cousins. It was fortunate the child died. Her friends would have been awkwardly placed had he lived, for they could scarcely have received her. It was surprising that she made so light of it herself.'

But Arnold had overheard what Mrs. Werner had whispered to Rudolph, and exclaimed exultingly,

'So! Is that how matters stood? The old lady deserves our thanks, even though she is in her grave, for the sins of her youth; without them we should have been forced to listen to some most insipid story, but we may now hope to hear something interesting.'

'Give over interrupting him,' said Flora, 'or we shall not hear a word. Now, Rudolph, do begin!'

'I am obedience itself, and shall be mute as a fish,' said Arnold, bowing gallantly to his fair enslaver. The male and female cousins all placed themselves in attitudes of attention, perhaps because they shared in the young officer's expectation of hearing some scandal, and Rudolph commenced his narration:—

There is little to be told of Aunt Francisca's childhood. Her father held a situation in one of the colleges, and the first eight years of her life were passed principally in close rooms, away from green fields and fresh air. Her father was much occupied, therefore her education was conducted entirely by her mother, a clever and amiable woman, but with one peculiarity, that she had the greatest horror of sick people, and was morbidly afraid of infection. Francisca, perceiving this weakness, determined to avoid it, but fell into the opposite extreme, and would scarcely believe that any complaint could be infectious, or if the fact were proved, she had not the slightest fear of it. When the family removed to an estate her father had purchased near a town where he had received a good appointment, the little girl took much pleasure in visiting the poor in the neighbourhood when they were ill, and administering to their comforts, which, of course, caused her to be greatly beloved among them.

It was at this period of her life that my mother and she became intimate. The cousins were much together, for my mother used to spend almost every summer at the Garlovs', and their mutual affection ripened with their years. At sixteen Francisca could not have been called beautiful, but she was pretty, with an animated countenance, a sweet smile, a light, graceful figure, and pleasing manners. It was about this time that a dreadful fever broke out in the part of the country where the Garlovs lived; it raged more particularly among the peasantry, but persons of all classes were attacked; the servants in almost every house were ill, and, to crown the evil, the doctors in the provincial town were seized with the fever. In this state of things, Francisca's father wrote to Copenhagen to request that some young physician might be sent to their assistance in the existing time of need. Little did he imagine that this letter was to be the first cast of the die which was to determine his daughter's fate!

Two young doctors accordingly soon arrived, one of whom was settled for the time being in the little town, the other taking up his abode at Mr. Garlov's country house. This latter was a handsome young man, about three-and-twenty years of age, who had just passed a brilliant examination, and was glad to obtain some employment. I will show you his likeness some day, which will prove to you that he was handsome and prepossessing in appearance, and that the impression he made on Aunt Francisca was not to be wondered at.

He was successful in his practice, and saved so many lives that Mrs. Garlov looked upon him absolutely as their good genius, while his lively conversation amused her husband. He had been a favourite with the belles of his own circle in Copenhagen, among whom he had been considered quite an Adonis, therefore he had no lack of confidence in his powers of pleasing, and he thought it his duty to pay marked attention to the young lady of the family by whom he had been so hospitably received.

But Francisca soon interested him. He found her very different from his fair Copenhagen friends, and then she was the only damsel with whom he associated; and in the country, as everybody knows, people become better acquainted in three days than in three years in town. It cannot be denied that as time wore on Theodore Ancker made rapid advances in the good graces of the youthful and unsophisticated Francisca, and by the time nature had put on its richest summer garb her heart was fairly in the keeping of the young doctor. Ah! what a summer that was for her. Never before had the sun shone so brightly—never had the skies looked so blue, or the trees wore so brilliant a green! And yet, had Mr. Garlov's guest taken his departure then, as he thought of doing, Francisca might have missed him terribly for a time, passed a melancholy autumn, and a lonely winter; but when spring came round, and the storks had returned to their nests on the roofs, she would have recovered her spirits, and remembered her intimacy with him only as a pleasant episode in her life. It was otherwise ordained.

It had been deemed that the fever had entirely disappeared, but a peasant was attacked by it, and in visiting him, Theodore, who had escaped as if by magic before, was seized with the dreaded symptoms, and soon became dangerously ill. The family—indeed the whole neighbourhood—were thrown into the greatest consternation, for Theodore was a general favourite; but no one seemed sufficiently collected to pay the invalid the attention he required except Francisca, who, calm in the midst of her distress, and heedless of infection, took upon herself to be his chief nurse, and waited on him day and night with untiring assiduity. Her father was often her companion in the sick-room, but Mrs. Garlov's uncontrollable fears prevented her from assisting personally in her daughter's benevolent labours, though she was not remiss in praying for the patient's recovery.

He *did* recover, and when the autumnal tints were stealing over the woods, he was able to stroll in the garden, or saunter to the verge of the adjacent forest. How happy Francisca was! And when Theodore turned to her, and said, in a voice still languid from weakness,

'How delicious the air is to-day! I owe it to you, Miss Francisca, that I breathe it again. Without your kind care I never more should have beheld these beautiful woods.'

A thrill of delight passed through Francisca's frame at these words, and she trembled so that Theodore exclaimed:

'I fear I am leaning too heavily on you; you are fatigued, I see. Let us sit down here to rest awhile—here, where the sun shines so brightly through the leaves that they seem to be all of gold. Ah! how good, how kind you have been to me! It seems to me as if my own character had improved since I became acquainted with you.'

The harvest was gathered in—the harvest-home was to be held—and there was more than usual merriment, for the dreaded epidemic had passed away, and the very last who had suffered from it, Theodore, was now only somewhat feeble. The peasantry were enjoying their games, and the Garlov family, with a few friends, were looking on at a little distance beyond the gates of the château, when a succession of fearful shrieks were heard, and a number of peasants, some armed with sticks, others with stones, were to be seen running along, though no one could tell what was the cause of the uproar. But presently a large dog, with a broken chain around his neck, rushed from behind some bushes, and ran across the field towards the Garlov party, who at the same moment distinctly heard the warning cry, 'A mad dog! a mad dog!'

Seized with a sudden panic, every one of the little group endeavoured to escape, and Francisca caught hold of Theodore's hand and hurried him towards the gate; but he could not run fast enough, the large stick on which he had been leaning impeded his movements, and, stumbling, he fell to the ground. Francisca was in despair when she found he had struck his head against a stone, and lay motionless; in vain her father called to her to quicken her pace, she would not leave Theodore. Meanwhile the dog came nearer and nearer—she could hear the rattling of his chain, as with open mouth and protruding tongue he ran towards them. She sprang before Theodore, and with outstretched arms stood as if guarding him. The dog rushed on her—she felt his damp paw upon her throat, his warm breath upon her cheek, his glaring eyes close to her own, and she sank senseless by the side of him she had endeavoured to save.

'Oh, fie! Rudolph,' cried cousin Ida; 'your description is too horrible—his wet paw upon her throat—shocking! How could she be so foolish! I think she must have been as mad as the dog.'

'I should have fainted at the first cry of the peasants,' said Charlotte, Ida's sister.

'Master Theodore must have been a miserable creature,' exclaimed Arnold. 'I would have defended the ladies to the last drop of my blood. But, to be sure, he was only a doctor, and dealt in potions and plasters instead of valorous deeds—that is some excuse for the fellow.'

'I thought the bite of a mad dog was always fatal,' said Mrs. Werner, quietly. 'Yet Francisca must have outlived it—how was that?'

It was a false alarm (replied Rudolph). The

dog was not mad. With that instinct which led all distressed creatures to her, it had run to Francisca for protection from the crowd of peasants who were ill-treating it. She soon got over her fainting fit, and Theodore also recovered consciousness, but the contusion in his head brought on fever, and he raved incessantly about the mad dog which had destroyed Francisca. The old doctor, who had resumed his practice, happening fortunately to call, ordered leeches to be applied to Theodore's head, and a certain medicine to be administered to him. Both had to be obtained from the apothecary in the nearest little town, and the only man-servant who had remained at home—the others having been permitted to join the merry-making among the villagers —was sent for them. After a long absence he returned with the leeches, but did not bring the so-much-needed draught. It would have been a useless attempt to send him back, for he had been drinking freely in the town, and could not be roused from the heavy sleep into which he had fallen after tumbling down in a state of intoxication on the floor of the servants' hall.

Should the poor patient be deprived of the prescribed draught? No; Francisca determined to go for it herself, even though it was getting dark, and she would have to pass through the dreary wood. Leaving her mother and an old woman busy putting on the leeches on Theodore's brow, she slipped out of the room and out of the house; she almost ran until she reached the gate which opened upon the road that led to the wood; there for a moment she stopped, and hesitated to proceed; yet the doctor had said that the medicine was of great importance, and though she had never been alone in the wood after dark, she conquered her fears and went forwards. But her heart beat wildly, her knees trembled under her, and she often started at the rustling of the leaves, and the pale gleams of uncertain light that penetrated here and there through the thick foliage from the rising moon; the scudding of the deer, whom even her light tread awoke, increased her alarm; and the hoarse cry of the owl seemed terrible to her.

'Young ladies,' said Rudolph, interrupting his narrative, 'is there one among you who will now doubt that Aunt Francisca could feel love?'

'Oh, Heaven defend me from such love!' cried

Ida. 'I would die of fright if I were to go alone through a dark wood at night.'

She reached the town safely (continued Rudolph), procured the medicine at the apothecary's, and bravely returned alone through the wood, though her excited imagination conjured up all manner of phantasies—such as dim figures gliding amidst the trees, footsteps pursuing her, and goblin laughter greeting her ear. Still she struggled against the terror that had almost overcome her, until, having gained her home and the invalid's chamber, she sank down, nearly fainting, by her mother's side, and murmured, 'The wood—the wood!'

The dampness of her dress, wet with the heavy dew—her exhaustion, and the medicine which she could just hold up—told the history of her exploit more quickly than her words would have done. Her mother threw her arms round her, and Theodore, who was somewhat better, and who was amazed at what she had done for his sake, exclaimed, 'Francisca, and you ventured all this for *me!*' During the long, sleepless night which followed, she heard again and again, as it were like the tones of an

Æolian harp, these, to her, thrilling words: 'Francisca, and you ventured all this for *me!*'

In the course of a few weeks after this event, Theodore being again quite well, found that it was necessary for him to return to Copenhagen. But he felt reluctant to leave Francisca, and put off the dreaded parting to the latest day possible. He knew how much he was indebted to her; twice she had saved his life, or striven to do so, with a devoted abnegation of self which only affection could have prompted. His vanity whispered to him that she surely loved him, and flattered by this idea, and also feeling grateful to her, he fancied that he entertained the same sentiments towards her. Francisca was so retiring in her manners, however, that Theodore had had no opportunity of communicating to her what he thought or felt, except by his looks; and even these seemed to alarm her, for she feared that she had permitted him to read too deeply in her heart.

At length he could no longer defer his departure, and with a countenance full of woe he informed the family at dinner that he would have to leave them the following day. Francisca turned deadly pale, and as soon as she could make her escape from table she rushed into the garden to vent her grief in solitude. Theodore had followed her, unperceived by her. He found her leaning against a tree, holding a handkerchief to her eyes, while her whole frame was agitated by her emotion. In another moment his arm was round her waist, while he exclaimed:

'What! weeping, Francisca? Are you ill? What can affect you thus? Is there any secret grief pressing upon your mind? I had hoped to carry away with me the image of the happy Francisca I have known here. Ah! you cannot guess how dear your happiness is to me. To you I owe my life twice over. I owe you more than ten lives could repay. Dearest Francisca! say, will you think kindly of me when I am far away? Oh, every golden cloud, every waving tree, every lovely flower I behold will lead my thoughts to you—or rather, you will be my only thought.'

Francisca's tears flowed more freely even than before. She was silent; but there is a silence more eloquent than words. However, young ladies, you all know, or have dreamed, of what might pass during such a scene, and I shall not, with my prosy words, attempt to describe what your poetical imaginations can so much better conceive.

It was under that linden-tree that the happy Theodore received the assurance of Francisca's love, and heard her, for the first time, call him 'Dear Theodore!' They strolled on towards the wood, and Theodore there took up a small quantity of the earth, which he said he would keep as an amulet—a preservative against all manner of witchcraft.

'Do so,' said Francisca, with a sad smile, 'for you will assuredly need that amulet. You are leaving me now; you will forget me soon among the many beautiful and fascinating you will see in the gay world. But, after all, you had better throw back the earth whence it came, Theodore. I would not be remembered as an evil genius.'

'Can you fancy that I could possibly forget you, or cease to remember all you have been to me? May Heaven forget me if I ever change towards you!'

The earnestness of his manner convinced Francisca of his sincerity. We are always prone to believe what we wish, and this is why a heart that loves is so easily deceived.

When he was going away, Theodore whispered with his farewell a request that he might be allowed to write to her, and that she would answer his letters.

'No, do not write,' she said; 'our faith in each other does not require to be kept alive by letter. We shall meet again.'

'In spring, I trust. Oh, how long it will be till then!'

Love and gratitude! What a wide difference there is between these two feelings. Love is the offspring of our own heart—its darling, its heir; gratitude is but an adopted child—a poor orphan, admitted but not tenderly cherished. What Francisca felt was *love*. Theodore had always *gratitude* starting up in the background to recall his wandering feelings; yet he believed, when he left the Garlovs' house for Copenhagen, that he was really in love with Francisca.

It is a pity that no natural philosopher has ever invented an instrument by which to measure love— its depth and solidity. Had such a test been available, Theodore would soon have found out his own state. But still there are proofs without philosophical instruments; for he who does not find the image of his beloved in every corner of his heart, has never loved; he who does not clearly remember every, even the most minute turnings, in the winding-path by which the little blind deity may have led him, has never loved; he whose beloved is not his all in the future, the object of his dreams, his hopes, his thoughts in the present, he has never loved. Ye gentlemen lovers! I advise you to examine your own hearts by these tests, and see how your affections really stand.

Rudolph paused for a moment—Louise glanced at him as if she felt sure he had passed the proof—Arnold indulged in a sneering smile, and the other gentlemen looked innocently apathetic.

There is an old French saying (continued Rudolph), which signifies that absence has the same effect upon love that a high wind has upon fire—it extinguishes the weak, but makes the strong burn more intensely. Thus, while Francisca's ardent love gained strength in absence, and in her sleeping and waking dreams she invested Theodore with every possible good quality and charm, his feeble love became more and more languid, and the image of Francisca lost by degrees all the attractions he had fancied it possessed.

Francisca had communicated all her feelings by letter to her friend, my mother, and the correspondence between them, on a subject so interesting, helped to while away the tedium of the winter months. Theodore, on the contrary, concealed his little love affair in the country from his friends in town. At first, it seemed a topic too sacred to enter upon, and afterwards he thought it would be ridiculous—he would only expose himself to be laughed at by his companions. Balls, and all sorts of amusements occupied his leisure hours. He was one of the best dancers in Copenhagen, and could have as many pretty partners as he liked. Time flew fast with him; he sometimes forgot that such a being as Francisca existed, and in a fit of vexation, as it reminded him of his duty, he hid away the amulet that was to have been so potent a talisman. Early in spring, however, he had an illness, which confined him to his room for a few days; during that short period of seclusion Francisca assumed a more prominent part in his recollection. Which of all the girls he had been flirting with during the winter would have risked so much, done so much for him as she had done? Not one among them. The country and Francisca were again in the ascendant for a time, and it was at this period that he had his likeness taken. He would give it to her. How much *she* would value it! That was a pleasant idea, for even in love men seldom forget vanity. Indeed, what love is to be compared, in general, to self-love?

Armed with the miniature of himself, and a small plain gold ring on his little finger, Theodore set off for Mr. Garlov's. The wood was already clothed in its mantle of green. How anxiously had not Francisca watched the budding leaves, and longed for the arrival of spring, which would bring back to her him she loved so much! She had gone out to meet him, and when he caught a glimpse of her, springing from the carriage he threw himself at her feet. She was happy, for she had never doubted his constancy. Mr. Garlov welcomed him as an old friend, but he did not look upon him in any other light, as Mrs. Garlov, who knew of her daughter's attachment, had never yet found a suitable opportunity to communicate the matter to her husband, though she was aware that he intended Francisca to marry a wealthy proprietor in their neighbourhood, who, although somewhat advanced in years, was a very worthy man, and would be a good match.

The evenings were still cold, and were consequently passed within doors, but were enlivened by conversation, music, and reading aloud, for Theodore excelled in the latter accomplishment, and also sang well. A happy time it was to Francisca, and even Theodore felt the pleasing influence of these quiet evenings; but when summer came, with its long days and warm nights, and the lovers could stroll out arm-in-arm, Francisca was still happier, and would sometimes exclaim, 'I could not have thought it possible for this world to afford so much felicity as I experience at this moment!' With her the days flew like hours, and the hours like minutes! At length Theodore spoke of returning to his home. But he was assailed by father, mother, and daughter, with entreaties to remain a little longer, as guests were expected, and his society would enliven the party very much.

'If you will only stay,' said Francisca, 'you shall be rewarded by seeing a most beautiful girl.'

'Is your cousin Kitty so beautiful?' asked Theodore.

'No, she is only amiable; but a Miss Angel is to accompany her, who is over from Holstein on a visit to my cousin. She is called Aurora Angel—two ominous names, are they not? But they are not misapplied.'

'Do you think I would stay for anybody's sake if not for yours, dear Francisca?' said Theodore. 'No; the goddess of the dawn of day shall have no such triumph. Since you wish it, I will remain longer; but I should only be too happy if this blooming damsel would stay away.'

She came, however, along with my mother and my grandmother, and very beautiful she was both in face and figure, with remarkably fine arms, and the prettiest feet in the world. She looked lovely as she played the harp, and her voice was one of that peculiar sweetness that, once heard, could never be forgotten. Her slight foreign accent gave a piquancy to her simplest words—in short, she was altogether a most attractive little creature.

Mrs. Garlov and Theodore Ancker were the only persons who did not seem quite captivated by the fascinations of the fair Aurora; every one else was enchanted with her, Francisca most of all. Theodore insisted that the glances of her bright eyes had, when she thought she was not observed, something sinister in them that caused involuntary mistrust; he accused her of being coquettish, cold, and heartless, notwithstanding her affection of feeling. In fact, he evinced a strange repugnance to her society, and much annoyance that the arrival of other guests had thrown a sort of barrier between himself and Francisca, with whom he could no longer be frequently alone, and more than once he expressed a wish that he had gone when first he proposed doing so. He was at all times a little given to variations of temper, but now he appeared to be always out of humour, and when he was compelled to show any attention to Aurora, he did it with a very bad grace, and looked as awkward as a dancing bear.

Aurora herself never appeared to observe anything odd in his manners, but the rest of the party could not fail to be surprised at him.

One evening, after Theodore had been all day looking quite cross because he had not been able to have some private chat with Francisca, though his own bad humour had made him neglect more than one opportunity that had presented itself, the little party were assembled in the music-room which opened on the garden. Aurora was singing and accompanying herself on the harp. Theodore seemed annoyed at the praise bestowed upon her, and she had scarcely finished her song when he began vehemently to press Francisca to sing. She declined, though she really sang very nicely, and her admirer was so vexed that he was leaving the room, when she called him back, that he might hear Aurora sing Clärchen's Lied from Goethe's 'Egmont,' which was then quite new. After preluding for a moment or two, with a sweet smile Aurora commenced the romance, and the expression of her countenance changed suddenly to sadness as she sang,

> Freudvoll
> Und leidvoll
> Gedankenvoll seyn;

while she seemed powerfully affected by the two last lines:

> Glücklich allein
> Ist die Seele, die liebt;

for her voice sank almost to a whisper, and her eyes filled with tears. At that moment her glance met that of Theodore, and she coloured deeply, while he in vain strove to look indifferent. Mrs Garlov entered on a disquisition touching the tragedy of 'Egmont' and the character of Clärchen, while Aurora sought to conceal her annoyance by speaking of the song.

'I do not know any song that has prettier words than these. Do you not agree with me, Mr. Ancker?'

'I think,' replied Theodore, 'that Clärchen's mother pronounced a very proper judgment on the words when she said, "Ah, it is the same eternal nonsense."'

'And I will answer you in Clärchen's own words, said Aurora, good-humouredly: '"Nay, do not abuse it; 'tis a song of marvellous virtue. Many a time I have lulled a grown child to sleep with it."'

This reply in her own language—the German—came so prettily from Aurora's coral lips, that Theodore did violence to his own feelings when he answered:

'Yes, "schlafen wiegen," that was perhaps Clärchen's art. Probably you admire Clärchen's character. I would swear that you did.'

'Yes, I admire it; it is a faithful and pleasing sketch of the female character.'

'Of *one* female character, say rather. God be praised, not of all,' replied Theodore. 'Clärchen is capricious, coquettish, inconsiderate, heartless. She makes a mere tool of the man who wishes to marry her—a mere hack and errand boy—and she repays the poor fellow's services by the coquetry which holds him in her chains. Does she not say herself, "Often, without a thought, I return the gentle loving pressure of his hand? I reproach myself that I am deceiving him—that I am nourishing in his heart a vain hope." '

Aurora listened to him with a smile, complimented him on his admirable pronunciation of German (a compliment which evidently pleased him), and then went on to defend Clärchen, quoting sentences from the drama itself, and wound up by assuring him that men could not understand love—at least not such deep, all-absorbing love as a Clärchen could feel.

Mr. Garlov remarked that the fair damsel was very severe upon their sex, and Theodore shrugged his shoulders in silence.

Again Aurora spoke. ' Clärchen,' she said, ' was placed, as it were, between Life's cold prose and Eternity's warm poetry. It was the battle between these that consumed her, as it had consumed many another heart. *You* have no conception of that struggle: and may you never feel it. May you never have to say, like Clärchen, " I am in a strange position." '

Aurora rose, put away her harp, and hurried into the garden. The other ladies followed her, and Theodore was left alone with Mr. Garlov, who said,

'You have got into a scrape, my good friend. One must be very guarded in speaking to these German ladies, they are so deucedly sensitive. I can't conceive, though, what made you fall upon her as you did; it was really an unwarrantable attack.'

CHAPTER III.

For some days after the little scene in the music-room, Theodore took great pains to dispel the gloom his ill-humour had occasioned, and he tried, by unusual courtesy, to do away with any disagreeable impression he might have made upon Aurora; but she appeared to notice as little his efforts to please as she had previously noticed his indifference, which had bordered on rudeness. He was annoyed, and said to Francisca, 'I can't imagine what that girl wants; I have never in my life beheld a person with so much pretension. If she expects that *I* shall approach her upon my knees, according to the homage she is perhaps accustomed to in Holstein, she will find herself much mistaken. One does not worship a pretty face so much in this part of the world; thank Heaven, here beauty is not so rare.'

'A face like Aurora's, however, is seldom to be seen anywhere,' said Francisca. 'But you quite misunderstand her—she has no pretensions, and hardly knows how beautiful she is. She is sorry that she is not on better terms with you, and, as Kitty tells me, cannot imagine why you dislike her so much.'

Such conversations frequently took place between Theodore and Francisca, but they had no apparent result, for Theodore, though he agreed with all that she said, and was polite to her young guest, did not seem to feel any interest in her; and Aurora, on her part, remained cold and distant to him. Six weeks had now elapsed since the arrival of the ladies, and the time had passed slowly to Theodore, who had never felt himself fully at ease; these weeks had also imperceptibly made a change in his and Francisca's manners towards each other —a colder and more distant tone had sprung up between them, they seldom met alone, and when they did, Theodore's thoughts always seemed preoccupied, or he was out of humour. Francisca observed this with regret, and one Sunday morning she contrived to follow him alone into the garden, determined to clear up anything that might have annoyed him. She had a book in her hand, probably snatched up by chance to lead the rest of the party to fancy that she was going to read in the garden. Theodore came up to her, and said:

'What interesting work have I to thank for this unexpected meeting? To see you alone is now a rare event; the claims of love, methinks, are no longer of the importance they used to be.'

He seized the book with some impetuosity—it was Goethe's 'Egmont.' 'Clärchen!' he exclaimed. 'Is Clärchen to be always thus thrust upon me? I wish I could as easily get rid of all Clärchens as I can of this book.' And he was about to fling the book away.

'For Heaven's sake, Theodore, don't throw Aurora's book into the pond! How can you be so childish as to be angry with a poor book? It was not Clärchen that brought me here; I took it up in the breakfast-room to have something in my hand; I did not even know what book it was. I came out here,' she added, timidly, and colouring deeply, ' to seek you.'

'Me, Francisca? Really to seek me? So these visitors of yours have not made you quite forget me? But I am unreasonable, detestable; forgive me, sweet Francisca! I hardly know myself what I want. It is very foolish, but I confess I am as jealous of Aurora as if she had been a man. The way in which she engrosses you quite separates us;

when a woman chooses to pay court, it is much worse than attention from a man—she scarcely ever leaves you for a moment.'

'Unreasonable that you are!' cried Francisca, smiling. 'Do you think you are to be the only person who is to be allowed to love me? Come, let us make the most of these uninterrupted minutes, and speak confidentially together. Let us go into the forest, I feel as if I should be more at my ease there.'

Theodore drew her arm within his, and they went into the wood. It was a lovely morning, the thick foliage of the trees formed a cool shade from the warm rays of the blazing sun. The birds were carolling among the branches, the chime of the distant church bells was answered by the tinkling of the sheep bells as the animals fed amidst the grassy glades of the forest, and a few peasants passed now and then on their way to church, in all their Sunday finery, and with their prayer-books in their hands. They respectfully and kindly saluted the lovers as they sat together under the large tree, beneath whose spreading boughs Francisca had prayed for strength on the memorable night when she had traversed the forest alone in order to obtain the means required for saving Theodore's life.

'This is our chapel,' said Theodore. 'This mossy seat the altar at which I have vowed to devote my life to you. Do you remember that it was here you hinted at the possibility of my forgetting you? Ah! Did I not then say that Heaven must forget me first? I feel now, even more than I did then, the truth of my words.' But at that moment a recollection shot across Theodore's mind which caused him a painful sensation: had he not all but forgotten Francisca? He passed his hand over his eyes for a moment, but Francisca took it gently away, while she replied:

'My doubts were unholy. I was but a child then, and I did not think that I could be loved as I felt I loved you. Forgive me for these sinful thoughts. I know now how true you are.'

Theodore embraced her, and played with the ring he had given her, which, not daring to wear on her finger, as the engagement was yet unknown to her father, she had hung round her neck, and generally placed near her heart, but which on this occasion had escaped from within her dress. Francisca had taken her own likeness before her glass, and, although it had many faults, it resembled her. She intended it for Theodore, but had never been able to gather courage until this day to present it to him. She had brought it down into the breakfast-room with her, and when she saw him stroll into the garden she thrust it hurriedly between the leaves of a book which was lying on a side-table, and took it with her when she went to join him. The ring reminded her of the little portrait, and, turning to Theodore, she said :

'You have been very kind to give me both this ring and that dear miniature — that likeness of yourself, to which I confide all my thoughts when I am alone with it. I have no ring to offer you in return, Theodore; but will you excuse its many faults, and accept this little sketch which I have done for you? When you look at this pale face, I beseech you not to forget that the soul which animates it is capable of the most devoted love, and is grateful for its undeserved happiness.'

Frightened at the warmth with which she had ventured to express her feelings, the poor girl became quite embarrassed, her eyes were blinded with tears, and her fingers nervously felt through the leaves of the book for the drawing she had mentioned. She found it, and with averted head, she handed it to Theodore. He kissed it as he received it, but no sooner had he looked at it than he exclaimed in great agitation,

'Francisca, this is a bitter mockery! I did not deserve this from you.'

Francisca looked at him with astonishment. He was holding the drawing in his hand, and gazing on it. One glance was enough to show her that it was not *her* likeness; the book had contained at least one other drawing besides her portrait. A young lady was leaning over a harp, amidst the strings of which one hand was lingering, while the other hand held a pocket-handkerchief towards her face, as if to dry the tears that were swimming in the soft eyes; beside her stood an elegant young man, in an attitude of utter indifference, cleverly depicted by his having placed his foot on a chair near, and being engaged in adjusting his shoe. It was only a sketch, but very spirited, and very well done. In a corner of the paper was written the German line—

Das Herz allein schafft Höll' und Paradies.

'Aurora!' cried Francisca, in dismay.

'Clärchen,' said Theodore, fretfully. 'Am I then

doomed to find that image everywhere—is it not impossible to escape it! Nay, Francisca, this is an unfair punishment. I have acknowledged my rudeness, regretted it in my own heart, and endeavoured to make up for it—what more would you have?'

'It is no punishment; it is only a mistake. I did not know that there was any such drawing in the book; the sketch is not by me—it is by Aurora,' stammered Francisca.

'Aurora! Did Aurora do this?' exclaimed Theodore, looking at it again, and eagerly.

Francisca did not answer, but she seemed as if she was going to cry.

Little heeding her looks, however, he remained with his eyes riveted on the picture; at length he said,

'Clärchen is true to herself. Only see what coquetry there is in this little sketch; and the verse, and the tears—it is really charming!—But what is the matter, Francisca? You look so pale—so overcome. Are you not well?'

Francisca tried to laugh at herself. 'It is nothing; I felt a little giddy, but the sensation has passed off. Let us go home, for we may be missed, and it is rather damp here.'

Theodore rose and accompanied her through the wood, while he carefully carried the book with the two drawings within its leaves. On reaching the house Francisca took it from him, and hurried up to her room. She put away her own likeness with very different feelings to those with which she had taken it from its accustomed place. It seemed so strange that fate should have made her own hand the means of substituting Aurora's likeness for hers! This incident, trifling as it was, awoke a degree of uneasiness in her mind; but she endeavoured to conquer the feeling, and, going downstairs, she replaced Aurora's book on the table where she had found it. Seeing, however, Theodore approaching from the garden, and not being yet quite composed enough to meet him, she hastily left the room; but, angry at herself for her folly, she returned after a little time, and with the intention of begging him to say nothing about Aurora's sketch, which had been seen by him without her knowledge. Why did she a second time so suddenly and silently leave the apartment she had just entered? It was because she beheld Theodore bending with the deepest attention over 'Egmont,' which was open on the table before him. Was it the play or the drawing which so fascinated him?

The old doctor and some neighbouring gentlemen dined at the Garlovs' that day, and in the course of the evening the whole party repaired to the garden; Francisca had quite recovered her spirits, and Theodore was in an unusually gay mood. Swinging was proposed, and Francisca and Aurora got together into the swing, which had a capacious seat. The old doctor insisted upon swinging the girls, but after trying it for some time, puffing and panting, he called to Theodore and gave up his post to him with, 'It is your turn, now; I am too old to go on long.' But Aurora vehemently opposed his doing it—she would not on any account give him so much trouble.

'Oh, I shall dispense with all gratitude from you,' said Theodore. 'Don't distress yourself about giving me trouble, that can all be placed to Miss Francisca's account; she will return so many thanks, that I am sure they will suffice for both of you.'

Francisca laughed, and so did the old doctor and Kitty. As if in fun, Theodore set the swing into more violent motion, and it flew higher and higher, with a disagreeable jerking movement. Aurora screamed, and then called out that she was frightened; but Theodore continued his exertions, while he exclaimed, 'Angels are at home in the higher regions, therefore it is impossible for Miss Angel to be afraid of reaching the tops of the trees.'

'I don't choose to swing any more; I command you to stop!' cried Aurora, with a look that made it doubtful whether she was in jest or earnest.

Theodore laughed, and then replied, 'Entreaties would have more weight than commands; you had better say *I pray you*, Miss Aurora. Now you can truly exclaim, "Ich bin ubel dran."'

Aurora would not condescend to entreat, but when next the swing came to near the ground, she prepared to spring out; in a moment, however, it was off again, and the spring, which she was then not able to check, was made from a considerable height. Francisca tried to catch her, and losing her own balance, she, too, with a wild shriek, fell forward. At the same moment both the young ladies lay stunned upon the ground.

Theodore was in an agony of terror; the old doctor clasped his hands in consternation, and Kitty almost fainted away. The rest of the party, hearing the shriek, rushed to the place where the swing was erected, and only added to the confusion. Theodore raised Francisca gently in his arms; he took no notice of Aurora, who still lay insensible after Francisca had recovered her consciousness. The latter was carefully carried into the house and laid on her couch by her mother and Kitty, and Theodore stood at the outside of her chamber door until he heard her voice speaking in its natural tones. He then suddenly remembered Aurora, and returned to the garden to see how she was. In the meantime she had come to herself, and had found herself surrounded by the old doctor, Mr. Garlov, and the gentlemen who were spending the day with them—the ladies had all disappeared. She tried to rise, but could not stand, her ankle was either broken or dislocated. Some of the servants were called; Aurora was placed in an arm-chair, and carried by them towards the house, while the old doctor walked on one side of her and Mr. Garlov on the other, the strangers bringing up the rear. Theodore flew to meet her, and exclaimed, with the utmost anxiety, 'For God's sake, tell me, are you much hurt? How do you feel?'

Aurora looked somewhat reproachfully at him, but she answered, 'It was my own fault.'

'It was the fault of that abominable swing—a most dangerous pastime!' exclaimed the old doctor, who forgot, in his wrath, that he had been among those who encouraged it. Aurora was carefully laid on a sofa in a small chamber leading into the music-room, where Mrs. Garlov and Kitty came to her after they had made Francisca as comfortable as possible; she had struck her chest against the projecting root of a tree, and the spot looked blue, but there was no other apparent injury. The doctor found Aurora's foot much swollen; the joint was dislocated, and he tried to put it in its place, but not being able to manage it, he called Theodore to perform the operation, which, though painful, Aurora bore with great fortitude.

The strangers, of course, took their departure, and the old doctor, after having visited Francisca, declared that he also was obliged to go. Aurora said she hoped to see him again soon; but he told her that he must put her under Theodore's care, as he would be unavoidably compelled to absent himself for some days. She seemed much annoyed at this, and anxiously requested to be removed to Copenhagen, for she would suffer any amount of pain on the journey, she said, rather than be attended by Theodore. She was assured, however, that it was absolutely necessary for her to remain where she was. Theodore cursed in his heart his past rudeness to Aurora, which had caused the poor girl to dislike him so much.

Meantime, every arrangement was made for Aurora's comfort, and her host and hostess were most assiduous in their attention to her. She happened, however, to be alone when Theodore paid her his first visit next morning. She lay on the sofa, which had been converted into a bed, in a white dressing-gown, with her beautiful hair falling negligently about her shoulders, and her rounded cheek resting on one hand. So beautiful did she look, that Theodore started on entering the room, and stood as if turned into a statue of stone; it was some moments before he could recover himself sufficiently to ask her how she was.

Aurora gave him one of her sweetest smiles, and held out her hand to him, while she said, ' Like the frightened one in the German tale, let me ask, " Daniel, Daniel, why do you persecute me?"'

This mild rebuke quite overcame Theodore; he

stooped and kissed her hand, while he whispered, 'O Aurora, be merciful!'

From this moment their former seeming dislike to each other vanished entirely. Theodore devoted much of his time to the interesting invalid; he talked to her, read to her, and before long had quite adopted her opinion of her favourite Clärchen in the drama of 'Egmont.' Francisca made no fuss about herself, but she had come off the worst, nevertheless, for the blow on her chest had brought on a spitting of blood, which, however, she concealed from every one except my mother—her cousin Kitty. Aurora's foot had had ample time to get well; but she complained constantly of it, and could not be induced to try to walk. Thus, at the end of three weeks, she was still confined to her sofa. During all this time Theodore had not had any opportunity of conversing alone with Francisca, for either the one or the other was in attendance on Aurora, or they were both with her. Francisca looked pale and ill, and ought by rights to have changed places with Aurora, who reclined like an invalid on the sofa, though her blooming face was the picture of health. But as she still complained of her sufferings, Francisca innocently charged Theodore to be very attentive to her—an injunction he was only too willing to obey.

It never occurred to Francisca that Theodore might fall in love with Aurora; and yet that was already the case. On her first arrival he had been dazzled by her extraordinary beauty; but looking upon her as a cold-blooded coquette, he had endeavoured to steel his heart against her. It was mistrust of himself which made him pretend to dislike her; her indifference piqued him, and was the cause of his ill-humour and caprice, but Francisca's mistake about the sketches awoke a new feeling in him, and he determined to win Aurora's love. *She* marked well all the fluctuations in his feelings and his manners, but, sure of her game, she went calmly on. Theodore had judged rightly when he had denounced the sketch as an artful piece of coquetry; nevertheless, it had its effect on him in spite of his sober reason. The particular attention which he always showed Francisca provoked Aurora, who could not endure anyone to interfere with the monopoly of all homage which she claimed for herself, and she worked hard to separate them. The scene at the swing and its consequences, though caused only by her jealousy, had aided her designs, and now she had not a doubt of her conquest. Both Theodore and Aurora were vain—both were coquettes—for gentlemen can be coquettes as well as ladies; the difference between them was, that she was a profound coquette, he a thoughtless one; she had improved her talents in that way by deep study, he was guided only by his natural tendencies. Surely much were those to be pitied who had founded their hopes on such characters, for they had built their house upon quicksand!

Theodore soon found that he could no longer gloss over his feelings for Aurora, and shelter them under the well-sounding names of regret, duty, Christian charity, or friendship, with which he had hitherto tried to silence his awaking conscience. He was forced to confess to himself that he loved Aurora as he never before had loved—what had bound him to Francisca was only friendship and gratitude; yet he could not but admit that she had bestowed her whole heart on him. When Aurora began to limp about a little, first with a crutch, then with a stick, and, lastly, with the aid of his arm, he found himself so happy with her, that he could scarcely sober his feelings before Francisca, who, still unsuspicious of any evil, rejoiced to see them such good friends.

But all were not so blind as Francisca: her mother and cousin saw more clearly what was going on, and they trembled for the moment when she should find out the unwelcome truth, if truth it really were. That moment came sooner than they had expected. It so happened that Kitty was confined to her room for a few days by a bad cold, and at that very period Francisca was obliged to be a good deal with the daughters of the clergyman of the parish, in whose family a death had taken place. Theodore was, therefore, almost entirely alone with Aurora.

One evening, about dusk, Francisca returned from a visit to the clergyman's family, and on the stairs she met a servant-girl, who was carrying a glass of lemonade to Aurora. She took it from the girl to carry it in herself; the door was half open between the anteroom and the music-room, and, hearing Aurora playing on the harp, she stopped, not to disturb her. It was Clärchen's song, and Theodore was singing a second to it in a low tone. It was so long since she had heard him sing, that she sat down near the door to listen to his voice. He stopped before the end of the song, and Aurora finished it alone. As she sang the last two lines, Francisca heard Theodore sigh deeply. 'He is thinking of *me!*' whispered Francisca to herself, 'as I am thinking of him.' Poor Francisca!

'Grieved unto death!' repeated Theodore. 'You are singing my requiem, Aurora.'

'And my own,' said Aurora. 'Would to Heavens I had never come here! What have I done that I should be so punished?'

'Speak not thus, Aurora; I alone am guilty. Why did I not tell you of my engagement to Francisca? Why did I not fly and leave you both?'

'Francisca is of an affectionate but tranquil character; she will forgive a temporary inconstancy, if she has observed it; but it is not probable that she has. It is not yet too late. I must go, and you will soon forget me. Francisca may yet be happy—but, oh! what a blank is before me! Yet I must away.'

'For Heaven's sake, forbear, Aurora! Leave me! No, no, I cannot tear myself from you, come what may. My life is doomed—alas! there is no happiness more for me in this world. But these vows—these dreadful vows—must they be fulfilled?'

'They may crush our hearts,' said Aurora, 'but they must be fulfilled. Let my hand go, Theodore—

you are engaged to Francisca; leave me—leave me to weep alone.'

'Dearest—adored—most precious Aurora!—how wretched I am! How could I fancy that I loved Francisca? And yet, shall I repay all her goodness to me by treachery?'

'Hush, Ancker, hush! You will kill me. Go, marry Francisca, and be happy!'

'Happy!' cried Theodore, vehemently; 'happy without you? How can you mock me thus, Aurora?'

'Perhaps time may do something for us,' said Aurora, with a smile as beautiful as the sun breaking through the dark clouds in a stormy sky.

'I dare hope nothing from time,' replied Theodore.

'Ah! do you not now feel the force of these words, "I am in a strange position?"' murmured Aurora.

'You are revenged, Aurora,' said Theodore, not without some bitterness. 'The loss of a lifetime's happiness is surely enough to atone for a moment's thoughtlessness.'

A deathlike weakness, which she could not shake off, had compelled Francisca to overhear this conversation. The first words had been enough almost to kill her; as soon as she was capable of moving, she rose and fled like a hunted deer to her own apartment: there, throwing her arms round my mother's neck, she could only exclaim, 'Kitty, Kitty, what have I not heard!' My mother too well guessed whence the blow had come, and she was not surprised at what was told her. The cousins spent the evening alone together, and when the family had retired to rest, my mother sought the wing of the house in which Theodore's rooms were situated. He was not there. She was rather glad to escape an interview with a young man, at night, in his own apartment, and in returning she observed that the door of the music-room was half-open; on going forward to shut it, she perceived that a window was also open, and she went to close it first. But what was her surprise on reaching it, and looking out for a moment, to see, in the clear moonlight, Theodore standing below Aurora's window, talking earnestly to her, while she was leaning out, with a little shawl thrown over her head. Kitty drew back hurriedly, but Theodore had seen her, and immediately joined her. He forthwith began to account for his being found there; but it was evident that he was telling a falsehood got up at the moment. My mother interrupted him by briefly informing him what Francisca had overheard; she laid the ring and the miniature on the table before him, simply adding a request that he would leave the house as soon as possible.

The next day Francisca was confined to her room by illness, which was given out to be a cold, and Theodore set off for Copenhagen without having seen either of the cousins. Aurora soon followed him, and then Kitty communicated to Mrs. Garlov the fact of Francisca's engagement being broken off. Mr. Garlov had never heard of it, and often, to Francisca's great distress, wished Theodore back again. A hard battle she had to fight with herself, but she bore up wonderfully under her deep disappointment. And this is the history of Aunt Francisca's youth.

Rudolph paused, and Arnold seized the opportunity of exclaiming,

'Why, we have only had a mere tissue of sentimentality as yet. What has become of the child, Rudolph, that Mrs. Werner was whispering to you about? You smile—come, out with the child, don't withhold the best part of the story from us—the child—the child.'

'Oh!' said one of the other young men, shaking his finger at Arnold, 'what have you to do with the child? Leave it in peace, poor thing! there is no use in recalling these forgotten affairs.'

'No; we *must* have the little affair of the child,' insisted Arnold, as Rudolph was about to continue his narrative.

Francisca spent some years quietly in the country, not mixing at all with the world, and only cared for by those who were immediately around her. My mother was her sole friend and correspondent, and she used to pass two months every summer at the Garlovs'. These were Francisca's pleasantest days, for she could talk freely to *her* of her own short and too bitterly lost period of happiness. Her sorrow and mortification had not made her either sour or melancholy, as you will perhaps believe when I tell you that she had two or three offers at this time which she refused. She was about two-and-twenty years of age when her father died, and as he had lived up to his income, there was but little left for the widow and her daughter. They removed to Copenhagen, where they lived on a slender income, but slightly increased by what Francisca received from the Tontine in which she held some shares. Often did Mrs. Garlov lament, for her daughter's sake, their altered circumstances; but Theodore's name was never mentioned between them. Only once Mrs. Garlov had spoken of him, and then she had wondered how it was possible for her dear child to forgive him.

But Francisca answered, 'It is so easy to forgive, dear mother. Let us not, however, again allude to him; it only pains you.'

Theodore, in the meantime, had married Aurora. When my mother communicated this event to Francisca, she determined to burn every little memento of him which she had treasured with the pardonable folly of affection! and 'Oh!' she exclaimed, as with bitter tears she made an auto-da-fé of these souvenirs, 'may he be as happy as my most earnest wishes would make him, and may every remembrance of me be obliterated from his thoughts as entirely as this last withered leaf is now consumed!'

About two years after his marriage Theodore removed to Russia, where physicians, at that period, were in great request, and made large fortunes. Kitty had heard that his principal reason, however, for leaving Denmark, was to withdraw Aurora from the connections she had formed in Copenhagen, where her conduct often gave him occasion to repent the choice he had made. They lived unhappily together; her coquetry annoyed him extremely, and the number of admirers whom she encouraged to be constantly around her was a source of daily torment to him. A jealous husband generally makes a fool of himself; when he has an arrant coquette for his wife, his doing so is inevitable, therefore the names of Theodore and Aurora were soon in everybody's mouth, and *she* found it as desirable as *he* did to escape from all the gossip and scandal to which her own behaviour had given rise. Kitty, however, did not relate these unpleasant details to Francisca, who only knew that her good wishes must follow Theodore to St. Petersburg.

Shortly after this Mrs. Garlov died, and Francisca was left almost alone in the world; but she sought happiness in constant occupation, and in doing as much good as her slender means would permit. When my mother married she wished her cousin to come and reside with her, but Francisca preferred to be independent, and continued to live alone, with her servant-of-all-work.

Theodore had not found the happiness in Russia he had anticipated. His fortune had indeed increased, but his domestic peace had diminished. Aurora cared little either for his advice or his anger, and had soon formed intimacies which quite consoled her for his fits of crossness. He also found amusements away from his home; thus they often did not see each other for days, and when they did meet it was only to quarrel. One evening, on returning home at a late hour, he found his wife was absent; she had left the house early in the forenoon, and had not been seen since. Next day the servant of a Russian officer called with a message to Theodore, to say that he need not expect his wife, as she had gone to Moscow with his master, and did not intend to come back. This was a dreadful blow to him, notwithstanding the levity of her former conduct, and with a sudden feeling of hatred to St. Petersburg, to which he had no longer any ties, he converted all his effects into cash, and embarked with it on board a ship bound to Copenhagen.

But he had a most disastrous voyage, the ship was totally lost off Rügen, and the passengers saved only their lives. Theodore found himself all at once a beggar, and this calamity, following so closely on his other misfortunes, brought on a dreadful illness. He passed six months in an hospital, and at the end of that time was discharged—a wretched lunatic! The Danish consul took charge of him, and had him safely conveyed to Copenhagen. But no one recognized him there; his passport and his papers had all been lost in the ship which had also contained his money and effects. There was, therefore, no refuge for him but the common bedlam, where he was accordingly placed. It happened, however, that after a short time he had lucid intervals, during which periods he occasionally mentioned names that were known, and this led to the discovery of who he was, and to his being removed from the bedlam and boarded with a private family, who received a few gentlemen labouring under mental disease.

Tidings of his unfortunate situation soon reached Francisca's ears, for it was the theme in every family where he had been formerly known. She had deemed him far away, but happy and prosperous, loving and beloved; she found him near her, but unhappy, deserted, and an object of that cold charity which counts every shilling and every farthing that it expends. She determined to see him, and to administer as much as she could to his comforts. He did not know her; she stood before him as a stranger, and as if from the hands of a kind stranger he received the various little gifts with which she sought to please him. For a whole year she continued to visit him daily, and it was with deep sorrow she observed that his mind was becoming more and more clouded, no thought of the past, no dream of the future, seeming ever to enter it.

At this time the landed proprietor, who was formerly mentioned, and who had been attached to Francisca since she was sixteen years of age, again made her an offer of marriage. He was rich, high-principled, kind-hearted, and well-educated. She knew also that her parents had much wished her to marry him. But Theodore required her care, and she determined never to forsake him. She had just finished the letter declining the offer so handsomely made, and saying that she had resolved never to marry, when the lady with whom Theodore boarded, and who supposed her to be a relation of his, sent a pressing message to her begging her to come immediately. She hurried to the house, hoping that some favourable change had suddenly taken place, and that Theodore would be restored to reason. But there was no such joy in store for her.

She found him sitting in a corner of his room playing at cat's-cradle with some twine and his long, wasted fingers; so eagerly engaged was he on his infantine diversion, that he scarcely raised his vacant eyes as she entered. His gait was slouching, and his clothes hung loose about him. Oh, how different from the Theodore of former days!

His hostess was sitting at work in the same room, and looking extremely cross. A letter and a parcel lay on the table, beside which stood a little boy, whose inquisitive and half-frightened glances wandered round first to the strange man, then to the unknown ladies, and lastly, to an elderly woman in a foreign dress, who was sitting near the stove, and who said a few words to him in a foreign language, apparently bidding him do something he was not inclined to do, as he shook his little head; he seemed bewildered by the scene around him. Francisca also stood as one bewildered, but the lady of the house proceeded at once to explain things to her as far as she could. She told her that the foreign woman had informed her, in bad German, that she was the wife of the captain of a small trading vessel from Revel, who had been requested to take charge of the little boy and deliver him to his relations, the address given being only that of Dr. Theodore Ancker, Copenhagen. All the child's expenses had been paid. The woman had conscientiously tried to find out Theodore, and the lady in whose house he lived had detained her until she could send for Francisca.

The letter contained but a very few words; it was signed 'Aurora.' The child's name was Alexander, and he was three years of age. His mother sent him to take his chance in the world, as she could no longer maintain him, and she entreated Theodore to take care of him, as *she* was now no longer a burden upon his means or a sharer in his wealth. Not a syllable was mentioned of her own fate—not an address or reference to her own place of abode given. In a postscript it was stated that the child understood Danish.

Francisca's determination was soon taken. Although the child was certainly not Theodore's son —although he was the image of his mother—of that Aurora who had blasted her happiness—she resolved to give a home to the deserted and helpless little stranger, and that very night the little Alexander slept comfortably in a cot prepared for him, and placed close to her own couch. The same night she opened the small box which held all that had been bestowed upon the poor child by his parents. In addition to his scanty wardrobe, there was a little parcel containing some papers in the Russian language—certificates of the child's baptism and vaccination—and below these lay a miniature. It was Theodore's likeness, the same that had formerly belonged to Francisca, which she had afterwards returned to him, and which had now passed from Aurora's possession once more into hers, and rendered its unconscious little bearer dear to her. She gazed at it long, as if comparing the likeness of what he once had been with the ruin he now was. Days long gone by arose vividly before her; she pressed the miniature to her lips, and then put it away along with her own—with the likeness of herself which Theodore had never seen. It seemed to her as if the meeting of the two portraits after so long a separation were the type of a future meeting between Theodore and herself in that bright spirit-world which shall haply be disclosed when this mortal scene has vanished for ever. She knelt by Alexander's bed, kissed the innocent child who had brought the treasure to her, and who had himself been thrown on her compassion, and at the same time she vowed she would be a mother to him.

But her adoption of him gave rise to many reports. Some said he was a poor person's child, to whom she had taken a fancy; others, that he was her own son, whom she had till then kept concealed in the country. Her relations, with the exception of my mother, were the most ill-natured. They took great pains to find out who could have been the boy's father, and finally had the folly to confer his paternity upon her old lover, the poor deranged doctor, whom she visited so often.

'Well, there was not such folly in that belief, after all,' said Arnold. 'For want of a better, I think we must accept this parentage for the youngster; for the story of a boy three years old travelling over from Russia, as if he had fallen from the moon, is not at all credible.'

'But I can swear to the truth of it,' said Rudolph. 'Do you doubt my word?'

'I do *not* doubt your word in the slightest degree,' replied Arnold; 'that is to say, I do not doubt that you believe what you have been telling us. But I think it likely that your mother kindly got up this pretty story, and impressed it on your mind to hide your cousin's little *faux pas*.'

'You judge of other people's principles by the rectitude of your own, I presume,' said Rudolph, laughing. 'But to continue:'

Aunt Francisca's prayers were not unanswered, for Theodore recovered his senses before he died. He recognized Francisca, blessed her for all her goodness to him, and passed into eternity with her name on his lips.

Alexander was a great source of happiness to Francisca, but severe trials still awaited her. He was carried off by a fever exactly one month after the death of her dearest and most faithful friend, my poor mother, and she was left alone in the world. The rest of her life was devoted to works of charity, for no day passed over her head without her being engaged in some act of benevolence. Love was an absolute necessity to her, therefore she transferred to me much of the affection she had felt for my mother. It was her delight to make people happy, and her last deed was to give what she knew would confer happiness.

'Good soul!' cried Arnold, laughing. 'That deed was to bestow on Mr. Horn all her lands and tenements—her goods and chattels—her Chinese pagodas and mandarins. I wish you joy of the inheritance.'

Flora turned angrily upon him, and exclaimed, 'For shame, Arnold!' But Rudolph went on quietly.

'I repeat, her last deed was an act of benevolence. None of us knew that Aunt Francisca had money to leave. She never spoke of this, for she wished to be valued for herself, not for what she possessed.'

'Aunt Francisca rich! You really must be quizzing us,' exclaimed Mrs. Werner.

'No; I only knew it myself this evening. It seems that she was the last surviving member of the Tontine, which I mentioned before, and she became, by its rules, the possessor of the whole sum. I hold her will here, in my hand, and I find that she has left not less than twenty thousand dollars.'

The whole party gathered round Rudolph and Louise, and poured forth congratulations.

'My dear Louise,' said Mrs. Werner, 'what a nice addition this will be to your income, and what a mercy it was that Aunt Francisca never married. Had she done so, Rudolph and you would not have got a shilling, though you were both so fond of her.'

'I loved Aunt Francisca for her own sake,' replied

Louise; 'and I almost wish that she had left nothing to Rudolph but the little matters she valued herself.'

Rudolph took Louise's hand in silence and kissed it.

'Good Heavens!' exclaimed Arnold. 'She has left twenty thousand dollars, do you say? No wonder you were her faithful knight, Rudolph! It was a sort of instinct that led you to take up that position; you scented the cash. For twenty thousand dollars I would pledge myself to sing the blessed creature's praises all the days of my life, and for half that sum I would swear to draw a merciful veil over the affair of the child?'

'Would you?' said Rudolph. 'Then I will take you at your word. Listen now to *the Will*. "As my dear cousin Rudolph Horn is so well provided for that he does not stand in need of what I can give, and as his marriage is not delayed by any pecuniary difficulties, I shall leave him only five thousand dollars from my Tontine capital; the other fifteen thousand I hereby bequeath to my dear Flora Werner and to Lieutenant Arnold, upon the condition that their wedding takes place within one year from the day of my death." You see that this bequest is a passport from Aunt Francisca to that happiness in the future for you two which fate had denied to herself. Perhaps you were so polite as to walk home with her some evening, Arnold, and that you entrusted to her the secret of your engagement,' added Rudolph, with a slight sneer.

Arnold coloured and bit his lips. Flora would not believe what she had heard until she saw the words on paper; and Cousin Ida, who looked over her shoulder, to convince herself also, exclaimed, 'Fifteen thousand dollars! There it stands, true enough. Who would, have thought that the old lady could leave so large a legacy? It is quite a godsend to you and Arnold, Flora.'

Flora burst into tears, and threw herself into her sister's arms.

'Well, recommend me to old maids, however absurd they may be,' said one of the gentlemen; 'who could have guessed that such a windfall would have come through one of the sisterhood? I solemnly vow hereafter to pay court to all old maids, for no one can know what they may leave behind when they are screwed down in their coffins. And if I fail with ten of them, the eleventh may prove a benefactress.'

'You have drawn another moral from Rudolph's tale to what I expected,' said Mrs. Werner; 'but your ideas are perhaps those which would generally suggest themselves in this selfish world. Take care, in future, to show decent civility to old maids. You will not, of course, do so from kindness of heart, but bear in mind that there is always a hope of being remembered in the last will and testament.'

Arnold sat for a few minutes quite abashed, with his hands over his eyes; at length he looked up and exclaimed:

'Aunt Francisca has heaped coals of fire on my head. She has humbled me thoroughly, and taught me a painful lesson; but I had well deserved it. You cannot conceive how much I am ashamed of myself: I feel quite guilty before you all.'

'Aunt Francisca knew how to distinguish thoughtlessness from malignity,' said Rudolph, as he joined Flora's and Arnold's hands. 'The slight annoyance you might have occasioned her was soon forgiven and forgotten. Be as happy together as she prayed you might be. I can add no higher wish for you both. But when you meet by chance an old maid, do not forget that you were—Aunt Francisca's heirs.'

THE SHIPWRECKED MARINER'S TREASURE.*

FROM THE DANISH OF CARIT ETLAR.

CHAPTER I.

ONE summer afternoon, two young fishermen were together before the door of one of the last cottages which are situated between the sandhills near Stadil Fiord, in the district of Ringkjöbing. The one was painting a pair of oars, the other had stretched himself at full length along the bench near the well, and was resting his head idly on both his hands, while he watched his comrade's work. In this attitude his countenance expressed a sort of quiet contentment, which seemed never to have been disturbed by the storms of passion. He had a low forehead, prominent eyes, a round face, smooth hair, combed straight down, and colossal limbs. His companion was of more slender proportions, and evidently possessed

* From a collection of Tales, in one volume, entitled 'Haablos'—'Hopeless.'

less bodily strength; but he seemed active, and there was an expression of benevolence and honesty in his features that could not fail to inspire confidence in him.

The sun was shining that afternoon from a cloudless sky; the larks were singing, gulls and other sea-birds were flying about in circles in the air; and the monotonous sound of the waves of the German Ocean, rolling lazily on the Jutland coast, as, borne across the sandhills, was like the audible breathing of a sleeping giant. The church bell at Vædersö was ringing for the afternoon service. All was quiet and repose in that sandy desert, where the eye in vain sought a tree, a bush, a single blade of fresh green. Only the lymegrass amidst the hillocks, and here and there a little yellow patch of rough, half-withered grass in the hollows, varied the dismally uniform colour of the sand.

'Come, now,' said the young man who was doing nothing, after he had remained a long time silently contemplating the other, 'put away that paint-pot, and give up work for to-day. Wash your hands, Jörgen, and come with me to Vædersö; we will have a game at skittles. This is a holiday, and one can't be always labouring.'

The young man thus addressed looked up and smiled, and after having for a minute glanced at his handiwork with apparent pleasure, he exclaimed:

'I am ready now, Ebbe. But only look! I have painted two hearts, with a wreath round them, inside of our names, which are to signify that you and I will hold together in friendship and good companionship all our days.'

'Yes, that we will, Jörgen.'

'I don't see why one should be idle all Sunday, any more than on other days,' said Jörgen. 'In spring, you know, we two bought a boat together; it was a very ugly one, and in a sadly dilapidated state, you may remember; but in consequence of devoting our spare time to repairing and beautifying it, we have now got as smart a little craft as there is on the whole coast. I am never so happy as when I am at work.'

'And I am never so happy as when I can lie quietly and comfortably on my back in the sunshine, and look up at the heavens, as I am doing now. I don't see the least use in a man's working harder than he absolutely need do. You and I, Jörgen, have been obliged to work since we were quite little fellows. Our parents sent us away among strangers, because they had no longer the means of maintaining us; we toiled and slaved for the benefit of others, and for the same reward that they gave their beasts —for mere food. From those days to this, we have never been able, with our united efforts, to make more than the fifteen dollars we paid for the boat. And now we must begin to labour afresh; and so we shall be forced to go on through the whole of our lives, until we are too old to work any more, and then we shall be thrust into the poor-house, as our parents before us were, and get leave to hobble about with a stick and a clay pot, to beg for food from those whom we helped to enrich when we were young. You may laugh, Jörgen, but what I am saying is the plain truth nevertheless. If a poor lad such as I am could only earn enough in his youth to enable him to take it easy in his old age, he would be labouring to some purpose; if our gains could amount to so much as the gains of the person who owns that large ship out yonder; or if we could make as much as the lord of the manor at Aabjerg possesses, who has nothing to do but to drive in summer round his fields, with his hands behind his back, and his German pipe in his mouth, and in winter to sit at home in his warm chimney-corner, and play at cards with all the strangers that visit him, it would be another thing. Ah, Jörgen, Jörgen! if one could only get so far as to be able to take the reins in one's own hands, instead of carrying the bit in one's mouth.'

Jörgen shrugged his shoulders and smiled. Shortly afterwards, the two young fishermen were to be seen strolling arm in arm to the village of Vædersö.

Towards evening the weather changed; the skies became cloudy, and before the sun had set the whole coast wore an aspect very different from the peaceful calm that had reigned around in the earlier part of the afternoon. A cold north-west wind blew in sharply from the sea, whose waves, rising higher and higher every moment, sent a thick rain of spray and foam over the adjacent sandhills, whilst the breakers dashed loudly on the reefs along the shore. The sand began to whirl about among the hills, and flocks of sea-gulls and other birds flew in towards the beach, their hoarse and mournful cries predicting bad weather.

The peasants at Vædersö had finished their games of skittles, and were about to return to their homes, when a fisherman brought to the little town the tidings that a foreign ship was in distress at sea, outside of Husby Sandhills. This intelligence, which seemed to interest all who heard it, drew particular attention from those who were standing in groups. A number of men and women set off immediately on the way to the sandhills, without heeding the rain and the coming storm.

Amidst the crowd who sought as speedily as possible to witness the calamitous spectacle might be observed a person of a very peculiar appearance. He was a tall, heavy-limbed man, with a blood-red complexion, the natural hue of which became deeper and deeper every moment, in consequence of the haste with which he was making his way through the heavy sandy road. His face was encircled by a forest of coal-black hair and beard, and shaded by a dark calf-skin cap. The deep-set eyes were nearly hidden beneath a pair of dark eyebrows that almost met over a nose which looked unnaturally broad, as chance had not bestowed much length upon it. This was the village blacksmith. He was by birth a Pole, and had served for some time in the army, under the reign of Frederick VI.

The road from Vædersö to the sandhills, as has been said, was entirely through sand. On both sides might be seen fields of rye, whose slender pale blades were beaten down by the tempest. The smith had taken as a companion along this fatiguing path a favourite and faithful friend, who lived at free quarters in his house, and carried on in this comfortable abode his trade, which was that of the village tailor. These two persons were almost always to be seen together—the lesser man, indeed, seemed to be quite a necessary appendage to the taller one, who looked as if nature had appointed him the tailor's protector. The merits of the latter, however, were not to be questioned; he was an untiring listener, and so submissive and dependent that, if the smith had pushed him out by the door, he would have crept back through a window; so complaisant, that if the smith had chosen to tell a falsehood, the tailor would have sworn to its truth.

These two individuals formed, for the moment, the centre of a group of peasants who had gathered on the sandhills. Below, upon the sea-shore, were to be seen several fishermen hard at work, drawing up their boats farther on the beach, and when that was done, standing in silence, anxiously contemplating the sea, on which a large ship was struggling with the furious wind, and heavy waves that were every moment driving it nearer to the land, notwithstanding all the efforts those on board seemed making to escape the threatened danger.

The groups among the sandhills were less silent. The smith had just declared, in decisive tones, to what nation the unfortunate ship belonged.

'Yes, as I have this moment told you,' he continued, in the sort of barbarous Danish in which he usually spoke. 'It is an English vessel, and I thank God it is not Swedish.'

'Why?' asked the tailor.

'Because they build their ships with such bad timber—only fir and pine—not an inch of good strong oak among it. I wish no evil to anyone, or anything; but if it be our Lord's will that a ship is to be run aground to-night, I am glad it should be an Englishman: those English know how to build ships.'

'You are right, there, Master Harfiz!' said the tailor. 'What capital iron bolts we got from the last wreck, and what excellent oak timber to boot! When the wreck that is going to be is brought to auction, I shall look out for a share of it.'

'And I also,' said the smith. 'I dare say, now, that craft out there will furnish me with some good strong posts for my new smithy; it does not look to be built of tinder or matches.'

'We can discern the goodness of the Almighty towards all mankind,' remarked the tailor. 'No cotton grows here—no silk, no iron is to be found; nothing, so to speak, but salt fish can be got on these bare coasts, and He is good enough every year to let one or two vessels be lost here that we may obtain what we require at a reasonable rate.'

'Yes, and He mercifully ordains this to happen generally in the fall of the year,' added an old woman, 'because he knows that the winter is approaching, and that poor folks want a little wood for firing to warm themselves.'

'There is no dishonesty in taking what is cast in to us by the sea,' said the tailor. 'They did much worse in old times down yonder at Nymindegab.'

'At Nymindegab?' echoed the smith. 'I know nothing about it. What did they do down there?'

'Don't you remember that true tale we heard last Candlemas at Thimgaard about the rich nobleman Espen? He lived at a castle which was called Ahner, and he used every stormy evening, and during the dark nights of winter, to ride over the sandhills with a lighted lantern bound underneath his horse, in order that the seafaring people who were driven out of their course should fancy that the light came from a ship sailing in deep water, and thus get stranded on the reefs while they steered for the light. This went on well for a long time, and Espen of Ahner became a very rich man, for all the wrecks on that part of the coast belonged to him. But at length, just when he was celebrating his daughter's wedding, a poor half-witted creature found his way into the castle, and disclosed their lord's evil deeds to all his vassals.'*

During this conversation the ship, which had excited the attention of so many, had tried several times to tack about, so as to get away from the shore, but the attempt had always failed. In the terrible storm, which seemed to be increasing every moment, it was no longer possible to carry such a press of sail as was required to take the ship out. Its fate could not, therefore, long be doubtful, as every swell of the sea brought it nearer and nearer to the dangerous reefs which stretched along the coast.

It is about half a century since the events here related took place. At that period the German

* See 'Eventyr og Folkesagn.'—*Espen til Ahner.*

Ocean had dashed many a wreck over the outer reef, and many a cry for help or death-groan had been wafted away by the stormy wind, or smothered by the sea, before anyone thought of taking effective measures to give help to the drowning mariners. On the occasion of the shipwreck in question, however, the unfortunate crew were often so close to the land that their despairing cries and earnest prayers were distinctly heard on shore, and the tempest had driven them within the outer reef, their vessel almost smashed to pieces indeed, but so near that, but for the fury of the waves, the fishermen could have got out to them even in their frail boats, and have saved them.

In the meantime daylight had gone, but in the summer evening even distant objects were still visible; and when the moon struggled forth from the heavy clouds, in the pale and tremulous light it cast over the sea, the ill-fated ship could be seen driving, with two or three small sails up, nearer to the coast. Presently one of the masts went overboard, was caught in the cordage, and hung on one side of the hull. From time to time, between the more furious gusts of wind, the gale bore heart-rending cries of distress to the land. All exercise of authority on board seemed to have been long given up, everyone apparently thinking only of saving himself. A boat was with difficulty lowered, but it filled the moment it reached the water.

The crowd on the beach was now increased by two persons—the lord of the manor from Aabjerg and his son. The first-named was a very stout man, muffled up in a thick great-coat and a fur-cap, with wings that came close down over his ears, and were tied under his chin. He had a tobacco-pouch well fastened to a button-hole in his overcoat, and was smoking a large German pipe. His son was a lieutenant in the Lancers at Kolding, on a visit for a few days at his father's country-house. He wore that evening a blue uniform, and carried an umbrella, which was every minute almost turned inside out by the wind.

'Hark ye, good people!' cried the great man, stretching his chin over the enormous handkerchief that enveloped his throat; 'we must try and do something for them out yonder. It would be a sin to let all these poor fellows perish, would it not— eh? What say you?'

'God have mercy on them!' muttered an old fisherman. 'It is too heavy a sea for any boat to live in; we can do nothing for them, Herr Krigsraad.'*

'Not if I promise a ten-dollar note to anyone who will take a rope out to them? What! Is there not one of you who will try it?'

The fishermen looked at each other, and shrugged their shoulders; but no one spoke.

'I shall add five dollars to my father's ten,' cried the lieutenant.

'Well, I think this is a very good offer,' said the Krigsraad.

'But you must not take too long to consider about it,' added his son. 'Courage, my lads! It only wants hearty good will and a pair of strong arms, and you will soon reach them out yonder.'

'Since the noble Herr lieutenant thinks so, he had better make the attempt himself,' said one of the fishermen. 'Your honour seems to have a pair of strong enough arms; I will lend you my boat for this venturesome deed, but I won't sell my life for any money.'

'The impertinent scoundrel!' muttered the young officer, turning towards his father. 'I wish I had him on the drill-ground at Kolding.'

* Krigsraad—a Danish title.

'For Heaven's sake be quiet, lieutenant,' whispered his father, 'and don't draw me into a quarrel with my fishermen. That man is no coward; I have myself seen him and another rescue sailors from a wreck in the most frightful weather, when there seemed no more chance of his getting safely back than there would be for me were I to try to wade out yonder in my great-coat.'

While this short colloquy was going on, a piercing cry was heard from the wreck—a gigantic billow had raised the ship aloft and cast it in over the reef; when the waves rolled back the vessel lay on its side, having been raised and dashed down again several times in the raging surf, and left lying partially buried in the sand. After this, every wave washed over it with a force that must have been seen to have been believed possible, and which, in the course of a few minutes, swept the deck clean of every object that had hitherto been securely fastened on it.

In the confusion which followed, another cry of distress arose, and those of the fishermen who stood nearest to the water, thought in the dusk that they perceived many of the sailors carried away by the sea, which, unchecked, was rolling over the deck. As the swelling waves dashed forward, these unfortunate victims stretched out their arms. When they retired, nothing more was to be seen: the men were gone.

Three sailors had crept up the shrouds, and had lashed themselves to the only remaining mast, and every now and then the wind carried to the land their agonized appeals to the people on shore to save them. Shortly after a boat was seen to be shoved off from the beach with four men in it; they bowed their heads, took off their hats, and held them for a few moments before their faces, while they seemed to be offering up a short prayer, then they let the boat glide out into deep water. The four men stood up, and appeared to be working hard to get over the inner reefs. For a short time the boat went bravely on, the oars were plied by experienced hands, and every effort was made to reach the stranded ship, but the raging sea cast them back, and filled the boat, and the fishermen were obliged to return without having effected their object.

At length, the next morning, about dawn of day, the storm seemed to be abating. In the interim those who still remained on the wreck had made another effort to reach the land in one of the boats which had not been carried away from the ship, but had continued fastened to its side. But this attempt also failed; the waves broke over the unfortunate boat, and relentlessly swept it out to sea. When the sun came forth only one man was to be seen, and he was lashed to the mast.

The Krigsraad returned to the beach at an early hour, and renewed his appeals to the fishermen. Ebbe and Jörgen were both there; they had not left the sea-shore the whole night

'The weather is not so wild as it was,' whispered Jörgen to Ebbe, 'and the sea is not so terribly rough. What do you say to our making the attempt? Our boat floats lightly, and will stand the waves better than any of the others.'

'It can't be done,' replied Ebbe; 'we should be risking too much—our beautiful newly-painted boat, that we spent everything we had to buy! You don't remember all that.'

'I remember that once when my father was shipwrecked up near Skagen, he was fastened to a mast like that poor man out yonder; let us do as the natives of Skagen did, and save him.'

'Let us wait a little longer, at least,' whispered Ebbe, eagerly. 'Perhaps the Krigsraad may offer a larger reward presently.'

Jörgen cast a reproachful look at his comrade, and said,

'God forgive you for the sin of thinking of money and reward at such a moment as this. I won't wait; and if you do not choose to go, I will get some one else to accompany me; for, happen what may, I am resolved to attempt the rescue of that poor man.'

'Have a little patience,' cried Ebbe, holding Jörgen back by his arm. 'Just wait till I take off my new waistcoat and my nice cravat; it would be a shame to spoil them with salt water.'

'What are you two consulting about?' asked the Krigsraad, going up to them. 'Have you determined to go out yonder, my lad?'

'We shall attempt to do so,' replied the young fisherman.

'That's right, Jörgen! you are a brave fellow, and have more courage than all your comrades put together. Well done.'

'I am younger than any of them,' replied Jörgen, blushing at the great man's praise, 'and I have neither wife nor child to grieve for me if any accident happens to me.'

'I also am going,' said Ebbe, in a doleful voice. 'I also will risk my health and my life to save a suffering fellow-creature. And though your honour was so good as to promise a reward, I must beg you not to think that I am going for the sake of the money. Nevertheless, I shall accept it, for I am betrothed to a little girl here in the neighbourhood, and the money might be useful to her if I am lost.'

'Go, then, in Heaven's name!' cried the Krigsraad. 'What! Do you think I am the man to withhold the ten dollars I promised?'

'It was fifteen, sir,' observed Ebbe.

'Well, well, fifteen then! Make yourself easy, I shall be as good as my word; but be off now!'

'I shall trust to your word, sir—and there are witnesses,' mumbled Ebbe.

Ebbe then divested himself of his new green-and-red-striped vest and gay-coloured necktie, which he put away carefully together under one of the boats that were drawn up on the beach. He then went down to Jörgen, who was busy launching a small, newly-painted boat into the sea.

'The weather is moderating,' cried the Krigsraad, filling his pipe comfortably. 'I think the sun is going to shine briskly.'

'Our Lord is pleased that we are so humane as to risk our all in order to save a human being who is a stranger to us,' whined Ebbe, as he took his place in the boat with Jörgen.

It was a moment full of anxiety and sympathy when the frail little boat was caught in the first heavy sea, was thrown up aloft, and then hidden among the engulphing waves! The crowd on the beach stood silent and breathless, and even the Krigsraad forgot his newly-lighted pipe. He mounted on a fragment of rock, holding his hand over his eyes, and standing with his head bowed forward, intently watching the treacherous sea; and he was the first to break the silence with a loud oath, when Jörgen's boat glided safely over the reef, and up to the side of the shipwrecked vessel. A thrilling shout burst forth at that moment from the spectators on shore— a shout full of triumph and joy; it rang over the waters as far off as the wreck, and Jörgen was seen to turn towards the land and wave his hat in the air, after which he made his boat fast to the shattered ship by the end of a rope that was hanging loosely from the fallen mast, and crept up by the side of the wreck.

The one man still clinging to it had fastened himself on the bowl of the mast. At the extreme end of the ship stood a black, shaggy-haired dog, who, with a weak, suppressed whine, was gazing out on the open sea, without taking the slightest notice of the strangers. When Jörgen reached the deck the man turned his head towards him, made a sign with his hand, and murmured repeatedly one word—'Water!'

'I am sorry you will have to wait till we reach the land,' said Jörgen, 'but, with God's help, that shall not be long.'

'I am afraid I have got my chest very much injured,' said the man, in the mixture of low German and Danish which he spoke. 'The same accursed wave which carried off our captain with it during the night dashed me down from the bowl of the mast, where I had lashed myself with the end of a rope, to prevent my being washed overboard. Whilst I was hanging there a heavy sea came rolling over the wreck, and it drove me with such force against the mast, that I lost all sense and consciousness. Since then it has been almost impossible for me to hold out against the weather, and I was on the point of loosening the rope, and letting myself go down to Davy's locker with the rest, when I saw your boat put off from the shore. In the name of Heaven, why were you so long of coming to our assistance?'

'We dared not venture out sooner,' replied Jörgen, 'on account of the awful storm.'

'Do you call this bit of a puff of wind a storm?' cried the man, scornfully. 'It is more likely that you were afraid of a wet jacket, or of catching cold. Ah well! I must not complain; you have done what you could, and I'm thinking that you yourself will profit the most by having saved me.'

'I don't know what you mean by *profit*.'

'Oh, that's not the question just now. Help me to get free of this rope; my hands are so cramped that I can scarcely use them, and let us be off.'

Whilst Jörgen was assisting the man, who at every movement that he made uttered a sigh or groan of pain, a voice was heard from the boat.

'Make haste to come, Jörgen, or Ebbe will lose the boat.'

'What do you say?' cried Jörgen, much surprised.

'I say that our boat will be thumped to pieces— to splinters—lying here and knocking against the wreck. Already the edge of the gunwale has started, and we have sprung a leak on one side; so come down, Jörgen—it is too unreasonable for anyone to expect that we should risk ourselves and our all to save other people.'

'A brave comrade you have got!' muttered the stranger, as Jörgen carried rather than helped him down out of the shrouds. 'Call out to him, and tell him that I have with me that which would make him cry his eyes out to lose if he does not take me safely from this wreck.'

Jörgen full well knew what effect this intelligence would have upon Ebbe, and instantly repeated to him the stranger's words. The object was attained, for Ebbe immediately came creeping up the side of the wreck, to assist in bringing the shipwrecked man down to the boat. The suffering seaman groaned repeatedly, and the exertion of moving seemed almost too much for him; bloody froth issued from his lips, and when he reached the boat he sank down exhausted at the bottom of it. The poor dog, meanwhile, had never stirred from its place, although Jörgen had done his best to coax it to come to him; the animal had turned his head for once towards him, and then sprang to a higher part of the wreck, with a dismal and heart-rending howl.

'There is no use in your calling that beast,' murmured the stranger. 'He has stood in one place and done nothing but howl since his master, the captain, was washed overboard. He will not quit the ship as long as a plank of it is left. Cast loose the rope, and push out with the oars, you there in the flannel waistcoat, who were afraid of scratching your smart little craft.'

After this petulant speech, the stranger laid himself back in the boat, and closed his eyes. Jörgen loosened the rope; as he did so, a wave carried the boat at once far away from the wreck. The dog was the only living creature left on board of it, and he did not seem to perceive that the boat was speeding fast away.

As they were rowing towards the land, Jörgen and Ebbe had a good opportunity of observing the stranger. He was a man apparently about fifty, partially bald, with a round forehead, high nose, pointed chin, and a shrewd and cunning expression of countenance, which was strongly marked, even though the eyes were closed. Ebbe surveyed his prostrate figure with a degree of veneration, and much would he have given to have known where the treasure could be deposited in safety, to which the unknown had so recently referred, and with the possession of which his humble attire so ill accorded.

The passage from the wreck back to the land

was made speedily, and in silence, until they had got over the innermost reef, which the receding tide had left almost bare of water; then suddenly arose a cry of exultation from the fishermen on shore. At that sound the stranger opened his eyes, raised his head, and exclaimed:

'What are they shouting for in there? Oh! I suppose it is in honour of the great feat you have accomplished. Nonsense! How far is it from this place to Hjerting?'

'About nine miles,' replied Jörgen.

'North or south?'

'South.'

'Ah, I thought sure enough that we had made a mistake in our reckoning; but it must be forgiven, since it was the last piece of stupidity our blessed captain has been allowed to commit. Are you quite sure that it is not more than nine miles to Hjerting?' he asked again a little after, as if the matter were of great consequence to him.

The two fishermen repeated the assertion.

'Are you going on to Hjerting?' asked Ebbe.

'Certainly; my sympathizing friend, it is easy to travel nine miles* with a severe wound in one's

---

* One mile Danish is equal to more than four English miles.

chest. Find me a hut to lie down in and a doctor to put plaster on me, and I shall want nothing more just at present. I have the means to pay you for everything you do for me. And now not another question or another word, for I feel the greatest pain whenever I open my mouth to speak.'

In the course of another hour the stranger was lying comfortably in Jörgen and Ebbe's hut. He had reported himself to the Krigsraad as the first mate, Fourness, from Amrom. Jörgen had gone to Vædersö to ask assistance from the smith, who, in addition to his other accomplishments, also carried on secretly the profession of a medical man among the peasantry in the neighbourhood. Jörgen found the learned gentleman sitting in his smithy, surrounded by some countrymen, to whom he was reading aloud the political intelligence from a soiled provincial newspaper that was lying, spread open, upon his knees. In the furthest corner of the workshop an apprentice was busy shoeing two horses.

When Jörgen mentioned his errand, the smith put away his newspaper with alacrity, and instantly gave all his attention to the report of the case.

'Do you think you will be able to cure him,

master,' added the young fisherman, ' or shall I go on to Ringkjöbing, though it is so much farther off, for the doctor of the district?'

'I'll tell you what, Jörgen,' replied the smith, in a raised voice, and with a look that betokened the utmost self-confidence, 'I will undertake to cure any creature who is not already dead, and even then sometimes they may be called back, as the worthy priest can testify, who knows that about Easter, last year, I brought back to life his brown filly, after it had been dead for nearly half-an-hour. If that can be done with a filly, I should think it can be done with a human being. Why not? But where is he wounded? In the head?'

'No; in the breast.'

'So much the better. We must give him something. I shall take my pills with me; if they don't set him to rights, you can order his grave to be dug. Come over the way, Jörgen, and let us have a dram together before we set off to cure the man.'

The smith then left his workshop accompanied by Jörgen. His secret — the preparation of these wonderful pills—it may be mentioned here, was found out some years later, during an investigation which took place before the magistrates of Ringkjöbing, on the occasion of the worthy smith being charged with culpable quackery. They were only made of rye bread and the juice of walnut leaves!

While Jörgen had gone to summon the smith, Ebbe had remained with the sufferer, who seemed to have become worse since he had landed, for he moaned repeatedly, and tossed about as if in pain on his bed. Ebbe sat by the window in silence, reflecting deeply upon the words of promise the stranger had let fall before he had left the wreck.

'What are you sitting there and waiting for?' asked the seaman, when he observed Ebbe.

'I am sitting here to see if you want any help before the doctor comes.'

'Yes, I want something. Get me another glass of grog, and let it be warm and strong. Do you hear?'

'It is not good for you, mate. When Jörgen went away he said you were not to have more than one glass of grog, and you have already drunk three.'

'You blackguard! mix me a glass directly. Don't you think I am the best judge of what is good for me?'

Ebbe arose and went towards the fireplace, where

a kettle of water was boiling. A bottle, half full, stood upon the table.

'It is too bad, when rum is so dear with us in these parts,' muttered the fisherman, while he mixed the grog. The stranger took no notice of him. 'I had to give three marks for the pint I bought for you.'

The mate still remained silent.

'Please to remember, mate, that the money spent for your rum was mine,' said Ebbe, in a surly tone.

'Oh yes, I shall remember it. Make yourself easy; you shall have your money back. What are three marks to me? I could cover you with gold, if it were not a useless expense.'

Ebbe's eyes sparkled, and he looked with reverence at the unknown, as he approached the bed with the desired grog. The mate raised himself, seized the glass, and emptied it at one draught.

'Ah!' he exclaimed, while his face was distorted with pain, 'that *was* warm! It burned me more than the confounded wound, but it will do me good for all that.'

'No doubt you have made many long voyages, sir?' said the fisherman, after a short silence.

'Yes, I have,' replied the stranger; 'you may swear to that.'

'And is that how you have gathered so much money?'

'What money?' asked the mate.

'That which might cover me with gold, if you liked.'

'Oh, to be sure—no, indeed! That would have been impossible. The money I own I could not have made myself if I had been as old as the German Ocean.'

'Mercy on us! How can you carry so much money about with you?'

'Who said that I carried it about with me? Blockhead! I have disposed of it better than that. The earth keeps it safely for me; I can take it when I want it; and I intend to take it up as soon as I am well. Then we shall have a jolly life. It has been long enough of commencing. But don't talk any more to me now; the pain is increasing.'

Shortly after Jörgen, accompanied by the smith, entered the hut. The shipwrecked guest turned his face towards the wall as they approached, but on Jörgen's informing him that the doctor had come, he muttered a few unintelligible words, and then stretched forth his hand, without altering his position. The smith evidently misunderstood the meaning of the action, for he laid hold of the outstretched hand and shook it heartily, while he said in a cheerful tone, 'Good morning.'

'The mischief take you!' cried the sailor, as he raised himself quickly. 'What sort of a doctor is that you have brought me, young man? I put out my hand that he might feel my pulse, as they always used to do at the hospitals, and he wrings it so furiously that I feel the shock through my whole body. Confound it!'

When the smith heard these words, which were spoken in the Low-German dialect, his scarlet face assumed a very benignant expression.

'So you are a German!' he exclaimed, in the same dialect; 'then we are almost countrymen. So much the better. I have nothing to do with your pulse, my good friend, and I should like to ask any sensible man, what use there would be in feeling the arm when the wound is in the breast. Turn over a little bit towards the window, and let us see what the injury is. If you are not able to move yourself, let me get hold of you, and I will turn you in the twinkling of an eye.'

There was something in the smith's sharp and determined way of speaking that seemed to please the stranger; he turned towards the light, and opened his vest and his under-garment. However rough and unsusceptible the three spectators might have been, they all started back at the sight of the frightful wound which they beheld before them.

'Well, what do you say to this?' asked the sufferer.

'Heavens and earth!' cried the smith, grasping his own hair tightly in his dismay. 'This really does look dangerous! I would rather have to deal with a horse in the worst case of staggers, than to cure such an awful hurt. The person who expects to set you to rights must indeed look sharp.'

'Of course you must look sharp; but only standing staring at me won't be of any use,' said Fourness. 'What do you think of doing with it?'

'You must have a good large plaster on it; and you must take some medicine. I have brought my pills with me.'

'The plaster with all my heart; get it ready at once; but I'll have none of your pills. I once swallowed a whole boxful of pills, and they did not do me the least good.'

'But you *must* take the pills,' replied the smith, decidedly. 'There is no use in jabbering about your past experience, my good man; you have got a nasty wound in your chest, as you see yourself, but you also feel ill internally, don't you?'

'To be sure I do.'

'Now listen. I know what I am about. A breast like yours resembles a watch that has been smashed almost to pieces. What would be the use of putting in a new glass if the works inside were not repaired also? So you must take the pills; and if you make any fuss about it, we shall have to hold you fast, stick the handle of a hammer in your mouth to keep it open, and so pop them down your throat. *I* know how to manage you.'

The mate felt himself too weak to struggle with his powerful medical attendant, and he made no further objections. The smith cast a significant glance towards the two young fishermen as he betook himself to the table, where he set about spreading an enormous pitch plaster.

'Come, this will do you good!' he said, when he returned to the bed to put the plaster on the wound. 'And see, here is a packet of pills. I shall give you some of these at once; and if you should be worse before I come back, you must take half-a-dozen more; they will certainly relieve you. I shall call again early in the evening.'

The wound was bandaged; and, after giving a few directions, the smith left the hut. Towards the afternoon the invalid became much worse, in spite of the remedies which had been applied. The wound burned under the pitch plaster; he tore it off; and, cursing and swearing, he refused to take any more of the prescribed pills. In this state the smith found him in the evening.

'How do you *really* think that he is?' asked Ebbe, who had called the learned man aside.

'Well, I think it is a very doubtful case,' replied the smith. 'Since my pills have done him no good, not to speak of the plaster, I am inclined to believe he is pretty near his last gasp.'

'Do you mean that he is actually in danger?' inquired Ebbe, with a degree of interest which was inspired by the thoughts of the mate's gold and the unpaid rum.

'When a person is ill there is always danger,' said the smith; 'and as he will not use the means for his recovery which I advise, I think the best thing either you or Jörgen could do would be to go and call the parish doctor.'

'You are right,' said Ebbe; 'I will go for him.'

'When you see him, you need not say anything about my having been here. These folks with diplomas are so very jealous. And I think you had better lose no time before you set off. And—by-the-by, Ebbe, you can keep the rest of my pills, lest you should be ill yourself some day. They won't spoil by keeping.'

The smith took his departure, and Ebbe soon after also left the hut, and set off for Ringkjöbing to call the doctor. Jörgen remained alone with the patient.

CHAPTER II.

'How long will it probably be before he brings the doctor?' asked the stranger, after a considerable silence.

'He will be here soon. There is a man who lives down at Væderso, to whom we have sometimes been of service, he will lend Ebbe his gig, and if the doctor be at home they may be here before nightfall.'

'I hardly think I shall hold out so long; the wound in my chest burns like a glowing coal, Jörgen, and my breath is failing me. Lord help me! Must I lie down and die now—now that I am just close upon the realization of all my wishes? For eleven long years I have been speculating on coming to this coast. I wanted to set up my rest here. I have plenty of means—plenty of means, and could live like a king; but first came that accursed shipwreck, and then, after I was so fortunate as to reach the land, to be obliged to creep into a dog-hole like this! There is no luck with the money—it is mixed up with blood and injustice!'

'What money?' asked Jörgen, in amazement.

'What, the devil! why that of which I am speaking, to be sure. But I will do some good with it. Do you need an hospital here, among these sand-hills? If so, I shall have one built, so large that a man-of-war might tack about in it. I will build a tower, too, with a lighthouse at the top of it, to warn my comrades not to approach too near the coast. And I will go to church every Sunday, and listen to the preacher, who tells us that we are never too old to repent.'

'How will you find the means to build these places?' asked Jörgen, simply. 'Bricks and timber are so expensive up hereabouts.'

'But do you not hear that I know where a large treasure is buried, that it belongs to me—*me* alone, and that I have only to dig it up in order to make use of it? I believe I am able to pay for anything I please.'

Jörgen shook his head incredulously. 'He is delirious, and does not know what he is saying,' he thought. 'I wish Ebbe would come with the doctor.' Then, turning to the invalid, he said,

'So you have been on this coast before, mate?'

'Yes, lad, that I have. Eleven years ago I landed

down yonder, near Hjerting, pretty much in the same way as I did here this morning. I am only afraid I shan't come off so well here as I did there.'

The sick man was interrupted by the opening of the cottage door, and the entrance of the smith, who said,

'I have come to tell you that Ebbe might have saved himself the journey to town, for the doctor drove a little while ago into Aabjerg. I went up there, and he has promised to call here as soon as he leaves the Krigsraad's.'

'Coming at last!' exclaimed the sufferer. 'Then I shall soon be well again. Tell him, from me, that he will be the cause of a great calamity if he does not come soon.'

'That I will,' replied the smith, shrugging his shoulders, and glancing towards Jörgen. 'Do me a favour, Jörgen, my boy. Just put my pills out of sight, and say nothing about my having been here.'

Shortly after a carriage was heard making its way through the sandy road, and the physician entered the hut. He only needed a quick glance at his patient to perceive how hopeless was his condition.

'Poor man!' he exclaimed, as he prepared to bleed him, 'you have been sadly hurt.'

'Oh, not so badly, after all,' replied the mate. 'Last year, about this time, the whole of the upper part of my arm was torn to pieces by the chain of the anchor—that was worse. You will be able to cure me. It is very strange that I feel such difficulty in speaking; my voice seems to be so husky, too! How long do you think it will be till I get on my legs again?'

'Why it is hardly possible to name a time.'

'The doctors here are good for nothing. In England they charge higher, but they know their business better.'

'Have you taken anything since you came ashore?'

'Nothing whatsoever. I have only wet my lips with three or four small glasses of grog; but it is very odd, I don't feel the least inclination for any more.'

After the doctor had done all that he possibly could to alleviate the sufferings of the poor stranger, he was turning to go, but the sick man grasped his hand, endeavoured to raise himself in his bed, and exclaimed, with impetuosity,

'You won't leave me, doctor? Are you angry at what I said about physicians? Pray think nothing of that; it is a habit I have got of amusing myself by teazing people. You must stay with me to-night —all night. Do you hear, sir? You need not be afraid that you will be giving your time for nothing.'

'I have not asked, and I do not expect, any fee,' said the doctor; 'but I have other patients who require my help as well as you. I shall see you again early to-morrow morning. God be with you till we meet again, mate!'

He left the room, and Jörgen followed him out.

'And will you really be so kind as to return early to-morrow morning, Herr Doctor?'

'Yes, my friend, I shall most certainly come; but, to say the truth, I fear that my visit will be of no use, for to-morrow your guest will no longer need my assistance.'

'What do you mean, sir?'

'I mean that he will be dead before to-morrow, and that no human skill can save him. If you should find an opportunity, you had better prepare him for this. Good night.'

The physician drove away; Jörgen returned to the invalid. He found him sitting on the side of the bed, the light of the lamp falling full upon his face, which, during the last hour, had become of a pale bluish hue. He was pressing his hand on his chest, as if to lessen the pain, while with a thick and trembling voice he whispered,

'Hark ye, Jörgen! Yonder, in the breast-pocket of my pea-jacket there is a small leather purse with nine Prussian thalers in it. Will you earn one of them?'

'I don't understand you, mate,' said Jörgen, much surprised.

'What did the doctor say of me outside of the door there?'

Jörgen considered for a moment or two what he should answer. 'Oh!' he came out with at length, 'he said—'

'In the devil's name, let me have no evasive answer,' cried the mate, raising his voice. 'I *will* know what he said, word for word; and if I give you a Prussian thaler to speak the truth, I think you are pretty well paid to open your mouth. So, out with it!'

'Do you wish to know the whole truth?' asked Jörgen, seizing his hand.

'Certainly.'

'All that he said?'

'Ah! it was nothing very cheering, I perceive,' remarked the sufferer, in a low tone, and with trembling lips. 'But speak out, my lad—speak out! Whatever that withered old stick could say, I can bear to hear.'

'Well, then,' stammered Jörgen, in considerable agitation, 'he said—he said—that you had not long to live.'

'Did he, indeed! Well, well, one must put up with that. A few years of comfort and pleasure are probably worth a long life of care and want.'

'Ah! God help you, and send you better thoughts, mate: you cannot look forward to *years*.'

'May I not? How long can I count upon, Jörgen? Speak, my son. Why do you hang your head so? I have seen death too often close under my eyes to be afraid of it. When did he hint that I might be called away?'

'He said that you would die to-night, and that no human skill could save you.'

There was a deep and prolonged silence in the room after these words had been uttered.

'To-night!' at length exclaimed the mate, in thick and trembling accents. 'I am to die *to-night!*' And as he repeated this dreadful sentence he burst into tears, and into loud, convulsive sobs.

Jörgen was much affected; he wrung the sick

man's hand, but did not venture to speak for fear of betraying his emotion. At length he said, in a subdued and sad voice,

'Take comfort, mate! If you will allow me, I will read a hymn to you.'

'A hymn!' exclaimed the stranger, starting. 'Ah, well—read it.

The young fisherman took a hymn-book from a shelf, and began to read in a low and trembling voice,

> 'Teach me, like autumn leaves, to fade
> With joy, oh yellow forest glade!
> A brighter spring is nigh.
> The summer of eternity
> Reigns where, an ever-verdant tree,
> My roots shall never die.

> 'Teach me—oh, wandering bird! like thee
> To wing my way, undaunted, free,
> To distant unknown lands;
> When here, 'tis winter, storm and ice,
> Yonder, an endless paradise,
> Open, before me stands!'

The dying man had apparently been listening to the hymn with earnest attention, even devotion, while his clasped hands lay on the coverlet; suddenly he turned towards the light, and exclaimed:

'Hark ye, Jörgen! If you will swear to me not

to reveal what I am now going to tell you, I will confide a secret to you.'

'Certainly,' replied Jörgen, who, shocked at this sudden interruption of the hymn, laid the book aside.

'Come closer to my bed—my voice is growing weaker, and pay particular attention to what I say:

'Eleven years ago I went as a sailor in a Neustader merchantman; we came from England, where we had sold a cargo of dye-woods, silk, and spices from Canton, and on which the firm, in whose employment I was, had made a considerable sum of money. Well, we were driven ashore near Hjerting, and forced to try and save ourselves in boats. It happened then like last night—the long boat was overcrowded; it capsized and sank! The captain had brought up his papers and a little box from the cabin, and was standing ready to go in the second boat, when an enormous wave washed him overboard. There were then but two men left; the one was myself, the other was the cook. We took the box, which contained all the cash for which the cargo had been sold, got into the boat, and reached the land in safety. This was at night, pitch dark, and in a pouring rain. Our first care was to bury the box—after that—'

'Go on, mate. I am listening to you, and I have promised secresy; you may depend upon me.'

'Well, then,' continued the man, apparently with a strong effort overcoming his repugnance to say more, and in a lower and more unsteady tone of voice, 'after that something happened—which I have regretted and repented deeply—something which I can never forget: after that I killed the cook, that I might be the sole possessor of the contents of the case.'

'You murdered him!' whispered Jörgen. 'God forgive you!'

'I did! But it was not such a sin after all. He was a bad, malicious fellow; he cooked shockingly, and was always making mischief between us and the mates. The next morning I was sent to my native home, and I left the case, well knowing that it was safe enough where it was deposited. Time passed on, and I went to sea again. First I went to Brazil, and then I went to the South Sea for the whale fishery, and so on, until full eleven years had elapsed before I had a chance of returning to the place where my treasure was. At length, luck favoured me, and I had determined to begin a new life, and to enjoy my money—and now, I am lying here in the agonies of death! But no, no—it is a fabrication of the cursed doctor's! I will not die! I once lay ill for fourteen months in the hospital at Boston, and became quite well again. Remember, you have sworn never to disclose a syllable of what I have told you. May God punish you if you betray me! Come closer to my bed. How cold it is this evening! Below the wall of Oxby church, at the corner facing the north, lies the buried case, among three hard stones. If I should not recover, you can dig up the box, and keep what you find. Have you understood me?'

'Yes, I have, perfectly well; but it is not worth talking more about, mate. I shall not meddle with your money—there could be no luck with it. Will you listen if I read another hymn to you?'

'Yes, read a psalm, Jörgen; it is long since I have heard of our Lord.'

Jörgen began to read slowly, and with much feeling; he was often stopped by his own agitation, and at these times he heard the dying man's breathing becoming thicker, and a rattling occasionally in his throat. He also heard now and then a sigh and a low murmur, which he supposed to be the invalid repeating what he had read. Suddenly, the mate laid his hand upon his arm, and exclaimed,

'I am counting about how much money there may be in that case, my lad. You will find much more than you can possibly make use of. When I was last at home, my brother lived at Amrom; you must send him fifty guineas. I know that they won't be particularly well spent, for he has taken to the bottle, poor creature! But that cannot be helped, it is his only gratification now.'

Jörgen nodded his head, and began to read aloud again.

'Oh, put away that book,' said the mate; 'what is the use of your sitting there, and reading that I shall go to heaven, and that I am tired of being in this world, when it is not true? I will live, and live merrily with all my money.'

A long and uncomfortable silence prevailed for some time in the room, which was only broken by the monotonous and uniform ticking of an old clock that hung against the wall. The moonbeams were streaming in brightly at the window, the storm had ceased, and the sky was clear and cloudless.

'If it should go hard with me, see that you have a large three-masted ship made with full rigging.

It must be painted black and green, with a red water-line, and my name, in large gold letters, must be put on the stern. I make a present of this to Vædersö church, and it shall hang there from the roof.'

One hour later, and the stranger was dead!

Whilst this scene was taking place in Jörgen's hut, Ebbe was on his way back from Ringkjöbing, deeply buried in reflecting on the unusual gains the last day or two had brought him.

'It is too bad that I am obliged to share all this money with Jörgen,' he said to himself; 'this stupid partnership won't do. I will see about getting rid of it, and carrying on the business on my own account. The foreign mate shall help me to manage this; he must have money, for he has several times alluded to it; he is too ill to leave our house for some time to come, and before he is able to go I shall have made something out of him. Besides, he owes me some recompense, for I helped to bring him off from the wreck.'

Thus far he had proceeded in his cogitations, when the conveyance stopped at the door of his cottage. The light was extinguished in the room; Jörgen was lying, fast asleep, upon a mattress stuffed with sea-weed, on the floor. He awoke as Ebbe opened the door.

'I have had bad luck,' said Ebbe, in a whisper, 'and have gone my errand for nothing. The doctor had driven out of the town an hour before my arrival.'

'I know that very well,' replied Jörgen. 'He has been here.'

'How is the sick man?' asked Ebbe, striking a light.

'He is dead!' said Jörgen.

'Dead!' cried Ebbe, in a tone that sufficiently evinced how many hopes and expectations that one word had overthrown. 'Dead! Good Lord! Poor man! Did he pay you the three marks I laid out for him in rum?'

'No!'

'Then it was a disgraceful imposition on his part, setting forth to me that he was able to repay us tenfold for all our trouble. Did you look to see how much money he had with him? I am quite convinced that he possessed nothing, and that he only wanted to make fools of us.'

'Now, be done with all this, Ebbe,' said Jörgen, almost out of patience. 'He did not intend to deceive you; and he was in the right when he said that he had the means of repaying us tenfold for what we did for him.'

'Really!' exclaimed Ebbe, with a smile, and a glance strangely expressive of covetousness. 'Then he *had* a good deal of money?'

'No; but he knew where to find a good deal of money. He had been shipwrecked once before on this coast, and then he buried a box, which, according to his representation, contains much more than we two could ever dream of possessing. He described to me the place where it is concealed.'

'To you!' exclaimed Ebbe. 'Indeed! Did he not say that you and I were to divide the treasure between us?'

'No!'

Ebbe seemed lost in thought; he remained silent for some minutes, while his countenance underwent an unpleasant change.

'Then it is you who have become rich—you alone; and I have helped to bring this about. Well, well, it was to be so. What quantity of money is hidden away in the box?'

'Oh! how should I know? Judging by what he said, there may be several thousand dollars.

But do not let us talk any more about it now. The cocks are crowing, it will soon be morning, and I am so sleepy. Come, lie down near me, and put out the light.'

'Several thousand dollars!' continued Ebbe. 'Good Lord! And all this money is *yours!* If I had not gone to fetch a doctor for him he would surely have said that we were to divide it. Are you quite certain that he absolutely said nothing about that, Jörgen?'

'No, he did not; but that is no reason why we should not divide it.'

'Oh, of course! You would be a fool if you did that. Dear me! Several thousand dollars! You will be able to buy a new boat, with an English compass in it. Oh, yes! you will be able to buy a house for yourself, and, moreover, to put some of the money out at a good interest. It is enough to make one mad. Will you spare me five dollars for a watch, eh, Jörgen? Jörgen! Are you asleep? Good Heavens! he can sleep! Several thousands!—and *I* have got nothing!'

Ebbe burst into a passionate fit of tears. The morning, which was then dawning, found him awake.

and ruminating on his disappointment, on the bed by the side of Jörgen.

The next day the body of the mate, Fourness, was removed to the hospital at Vædersö, to be buried from thence in the village churchyard. Jörgen and Ebbe pursued their accustomed occupations. The hull of the foreign vessel was carried out to sea at night, and apparently knocked to pieces by the waves, for many portions of the wreck were cast ashore along the adjacent coast.

Ebbe did not leave Jörgen's side that day; all his thoughts were devoted to the mysterious casket, and to the painful reflection that Jörgen alone was aware of the spot where it was concealed, consequently was master of its valuable contents. He had no inclination to work, but was continually recurring to the one vexatious fancy, which represented Jörgen surrounded with wealth and all the prosperity which he had so often wished for himself.

Thus passed the week. It had been settled between the two friends that on Saturday they would set off to Oxby church, so early that they might reach the place that evening, before it began to get dark. Ebbe had two or three days beforehand arranged everything for this journey, secretly and eagerly. Jörgen could not help observing the striking change which in a few days had come over him. He saw how his energies were quite paralyzed beneath the dreamy state into which he had fallen. Ebbe had become silent and irritable; he avoided his comrade's society, and sought solitude, where it was not necessary for him to conceal his feelings.

When he was alone, his mind always dwelt upon the hidden treasure, and picture after picture arose from the depths of his imagination of wealth, prosperity, and triumph over those who now looked down upon him. At other times he was tormented by a bitter, gnawing doubt if the mate had spoken the truth, and there existed any treasure at all. Then, again, he would make himself miserable about the portion of it that he might obtain. He would sometimes fancy himself set aside by Jörgen; then he would work himself up to believe that it was no freewill offer to share with him, but a right which belonged to himself; and to this oft-recurring thought succeeded, little by little, another, dark and dreadful, which, nourished by envy and covetousness, assumed by degrees a more distinct and decided form.

When Saturday arrived, Ebbe rose in the grey of the morning, and was ready for the journey long before Jörgen; his whole bearing betrayed a degree of feverish impatience, an eagerness and impetuosity which he had never evinced before. Jörgen carried a saddle-bag with provisions, Ebbe a spade, and furnished with these necessaries, they left their hut, and passed through the village even before the peasants had left their beds.

The road from Aale parsonage down to Oxby traverses a long and wide tract of boggy land, which, at that time, was overgrown with a sort of close rough glass and a layer of moss, that in summer concealed many a cavity and break in the ground, and which was the resort of frogs and of various moor fowls, that took wing in large flocks when anyone approached their places of shelter.

The two fishermen trudged on with unwearying patience towards their goal, which already they could perceive far in the distance. It was late in the day; the sun had sunk behind the line of sand-hills which hid the German Ocean, and a deep stillness reigned around. The church stood in a naked, sandy plain, surrounded by a stone wall that was partially sunk in the sand. One side of the edifice was, at that moment, illuminated by a bright reflexion from the red evening sky. Swallows were flying about under its roof. As far as the eye could reach, there was no sign or appearance of the inhabitants of the neighbourhood.

'At last we have reached our destination!' exclaimed Ebbe, as, tired and gasping for breath, he threw himself down on a heap of gravel at a little distance from the wall of the churchyard.

'Yes, at last,' replied Jögen, with a smile; 'and it will soon be seen if we have not had our trouble for nothing.'

'Oh, don't say so, Jörgen,' cried Ebbe. 'How could such an idea enter your head? You have surely not forgotten the place where we were to dig?'

'Oh, no!' replied Jörgen. 'The direction was not so difficult to remember. It was towards the north, he said, and among three stones which had fallen there from the wall. If you will remain here to rest yourself, I will go at once and try and find the place.'

'No!' said Ebbe, rising quickly from his recumbent position. 'I will go with you. Why should I stay behind, and not help you to look for it?'

Jörgen then led the way, proceeding along the wall of the churchyard, while Ebbe followed him with the spade over his shoulder; but it was some time before they found the place indicated. The grass grew so high near the churchyard wall, that, in the increasing dusk of the evening, it would have been impossible to have discovered the stones described until close upon them. In the time, too, which had elapsed since the treasure was buried, the stones might have sunk into the ground, or become hidden by moss. At length, however, Jörgen found the spot. The three stones lay exactly in the position the mate had described; a young elder-tree had shot up its straight branches just before them.

'It must be here,' said Ebbe; 'you have good luck with you in everything. Let us begin to dig at once. But, hush! be still! I'll be sworn I heard a horse panting on the other side of the churchyard wall. We will wait a little before we begin.'

'Let us rather go round, and see if anyone is there,' said Jörgen, about to go.

'No, by no means; stay with me, I don't fancy being alone in such a place as this. They say the Evil One goes riding about at night on a white horse. Have you never heard that?'

'Yes; but what have we to do with him? We are here on a lawful errand, and have no reason to be afraid of anything.'

So saying, Jörgen walked on by the churchyard wall until he came to the next corner. 'There is nothing to be seen,' he said, when he returned. 'Let us commence the digging. Lend me the spade.'

'No; let us dig by turns, and I will go to work first,' replied Ebbe, as he took off his jacket, and put the spade into the ground.

The uppermost layer of earth among the stones was hard and stiff, and moreover, the roots of the elder-tree formed a sort of tough piece of network among the stones, so that it was not possible to proceed otherwise than slowly with the work. Ebbe groaned; his impatience was increased by the strong spirit of covetousness which had taken possession of him. Jörgen sat down quietly on a stone near him. In the deep stillness which reigned around the spot, the bats might be heard flapping their wings as they fluttered about the walls of the church, and in the distance a hollow, rushing sound, which came from the German Ocean, away behind the sandhills. Ebbe continued to dig, and had made a tolerably deep hole, when he suddenly stopped, pushed the spade well into the ground, and bowed his head down as if he were listening to something.

'Do you think you have come to anything?' asked Jörgen.

'No, it is only a stone which lies in the way; but I am tired now.'

'Then let me take my turn of digging,' said Jörgen.

'Let us rather rest a little while, and take a mouthful of our provisions and a drop from our flask. What have you done with the wallet?'

'I left it at the gravel pit yonder, where we rested first.'

'Then let us go there, Jörgen. After we have had something to eat we shall set to work again. It will be long before it is daylight; we have time enough.'

Jörgen made no opposition to this arrangement; he was accustomed to give way to Ebbe's wishes, and he went back to where they had left their provender.

Ebbe cast a longing look back at the hole; then took the spade under his arm and followed Jörgen.

At a little distance from the walls of the churchyard the path lay near the edge of a pit, from which the peasants dug up gravel for the repairs that were annually made in the high road. The pit was tolerably deep, and sloped from the brink, along which the two fishermen directed their steps until they came to a kind of gap, or narrow defile, from whence the gravel was carted away.

When Ebbe reached this place, he took up the flask, drank off its contents, and let it drop quietly into the grass. Jörgen, in the meantime, had sat down, and began to eat. Ebbe remained standing, and leaned upon the spade.

'Why don't you sit down?' asked Jörgen.

'Because the grass is wet.'

'Where is the flask? I don't see it.'

'You will find it on the grass.'

Jörgen stooped down to look for it, and at that moment Ebbe lifted the spade, and, exerting all his strength, struck Jörgen with it on his head!

The attack was made so unexpectedly and so hurriedly, that it was not possible for Jörgen to avoid the blow or to defend himself. He uttered a low cry, stretched out his arms, and sank backwards to the ground. Ebbe bent over him, and listened. The blow must have been a very severe one, for he did not hear the faintest breathing from Jörgen.

'You have got this because you tried to cheat me, and packed me off to the town, that you alone might benefit by the stranger's treasure.' And, as if his bitter feelings were increased by this remembrance, he added, triumphantly, 'You asserted that it was to you alone the stranger had bequeathed his money. You would only have given me a small portion of it; I shall take it all now. And you did not know that I have already got it. I heard the ground reverberate under the spade—I heard the sound of the gold—it is mine—all—all mine!'

As he said this, he took up his comrade's body in his arms, and flung it over the edge into the pit.

'And now to go back to the churchyard!' he exclaimed. 'I must have the money up, and be off before the dawn of day.'

He threw the spade across his shoulders, took up the wallet, and turned to leave the place.

At that moment he fancied that he heard footsteps near: he looked round, and perceived in the twilight a tall figure in a flowing mantle, which stopped at a little distance from the place where he was standing. In the extreme terror which seized him, it seemed to him that this figure gradually grew taller and larger, and that it gazed at him with a dark and threatening aspect; it seemed to approach nearer. It was no longer a phantom of the imagination; he heard the heavy steps ringing on the ground —he beheld a hand stretched out towards him—and then fell, in accusing accents on his ear, the dreadful word 'Murderer!'

Ebbe uttered a loud cry, he dropped the spade, sprang to one side, and fled in a direction quite opposite to that where he had so recently sought for the unlucky treasure. He constantly thought that his unknown pursuer was still following him, that he was gaining upon him, and even that he felt his breath close behind him; but he dared not turn his head, he only continued to run swiftly, and without stopping, until at length he stumbled, and fell into one of the many hollows that were to be met with in that neighbourhood. There he lay for several hours exhausted and insensible, unwitting of the storm from the German Ocean that was raging among the sandhills near its shores. When at last he re-recovered to consciousness, the morning sun was shining on the sandhills, and he heard the bells of Oxby church ringing for the early service.

Eight days later, the inhabitants of Vædersö were thronging round a carriage which was passing through the little town. The front seat was occupied by a tall man, under whose overcoat was to be seen the stiff embroidered collar of a uniform. His self-important air, also the condescending nod with which he acknowledged the respectful obeisances of the peasantry, betokened a person of no small consequence. Nor was there any mistake in this, for he was the judge of the district, who was proceeding on official duty to the sandhills.

In the back seat of the carriage sat two men, one of whom was the smith of the village, the other a pale, emaciated, shrunken figure, in whose features it would have been difficult to have recognized Ebbe, so great was the change that the last eight days had wrought in him.

The smith's plump round face evinced, on the contrary, a great degree of self-complacency; he smiled to everyone he knew, and stretched out by turns his hand or his head from the carriage, either for a friendly salutation, or to explain the reason of his appearance in the carriage on that particular occasion.

The carriage passed through the village, and did

not stop until it reached the cottage which Jörgen and Ebbe had occupied conjointly. Here the judge got out, and after saying a few words to the smith, he entered the house.

'Now, Ebbe,' said the smith, 'you must get out too; you are at home here. We shall have a legal examination, as his honour has just very properly declared.'

Ebbe made no reply; he seemed to have fallen into a state of speechless apathy. He descended from the carriage, and followed the smith into the first of the two rooms into which the hut was divided.

On entering the cottage, they found the judge, and two fishermen who had been summoned as witnesses, already seated near the table. Ebbe cast a rapid and reconnoitring look around him; he perceived that everything was in its usual place; it was not the room that had changed in these eight days.

'Place yourself at the end of the table,' said the judge. 'Listen to what will be said, and answer minutely and truthfully the questions we shall put to you. Speak first, smith. Let us hear what you have to say.'

Not to fatigue the reader with the smith's long-winded story, we shall as briefly as possible relate the substance of his communication.

However important it was to Ebbe to maintain inviolable secresy relative to the mate's hidden treasure, he had let fall some words which had been caught up by the smith, and which, giving rise to some conjectures and suspicions, caused the clear-sighted man to watch narrowly the movements of the two young fishermen. On the same day that Jörgen and Ebbe had left their home at such an early hour, the smith had borrowed a horse from one of his neighbours, and set out in pursuit of them, although he took all possible pains to avoid being seen by them. Jörgen had previously given out that he was going to take a holiday to visit his aunt at Oxby.

When the smith had followed the two wayfarers as far as Aale church, and assured himself that they were really going to the place mentioned, he quitted the footpath, which, leading through the open heath, would have made him run the risk of being observed, and rode another way until he reached the cross road near Oxby church, and the shades of evening began to fall. The fishermen had evidently taken a considerable time to cross the wide heath. The smith had waited long, and had ridden around the church before he saw Ebbe and Jörgen looking for the spot with the three stones.

It was his horse that Ebbe had heard neigh, but, as we have seen, he had not sufficiently followed up the circumstance. In consequence of this neglect on his part, the smith became acquainted with all that was going on; for when it grew darker he ventured nearer, got over the wall, and crept on his hands and knees close to the place where Ebbe was digging. Arrived there, he could hear every word that was spoken while the work proceeded. When they left the wall of the churchyard, he followed them at some distance along the path that led to the gravel-pits, and he had seen Jörgen fall. Ebbe had not recognized the voice of the smith in that which called after him, nor had he observed that Harfiz was carrying Jörgen in his arms to the nearest dwelling.

'Thus it all happened,' said the plaintiff, in the corrupt language in which he spoke. 'Ebbe cannot deny a word that I have said. I know all that passed; I saw and heard all. I took up the spade with which he had struck Jörgen, and, to wind up, your honour has only to make inquiry here to be convinced of the truth of what I assert. Here you behold the man who can corroborate my statement.'

As he said these words he drew aside a curtain that had concealed an alcove, and Jörgen, with his head bound up, pale and suffering, was seen raising himself with difficulty on one arm, and gazing at those assembled in the hut. This last action of the smith, so sudden and unexpected, caused a great sensation and much surprise among those present.

Ebbe, who up to this moment had stood silent and immovable, with his hands folded and his eyes cast down, raised his head quickly, and when his glance fell on Jörgen, he stretched out his arms towards him, and, bursting into tears, exclaimed:

'Oh, my God! Jörgen—dear Jörgen!'

'Yes, there you see a competent witness. I have cured him—I may safely declare—and now he will confirm what I have said.'

'Well, what have you to say to what the smith has just been telling us?'

'I say that he is quite mistaken,' replied Jörgen. 'Ebbe had no wish to kill me; he had no evil intention against me; I absolve him of anything of the kind.'

Everyone was taken by surprise, and exclamations of astonishment followed these words, which were uttered in a mild, quiet, but at the same time decisive tone. Ebbe's eyes sparkled. The smith jumped up.

'Jörgen,' he cried, 'are you out of your mind? You cannot be in your right senses if you speak in this way. Did he not attempt to murder you? Did I not see and hear it all myself? Did I not take you up in my strong arms, when he cast you down into the gravel-pit?'

'You did, indeed, behave most kindly and humanely to me,' replied Jörgen, with a grateful smile. 'Without your help, I should most probably have been dead now; but, I repeat that it was not Ebbe who threw me into the pit. I fell in, sir, and in my fall I hurt myself with the spade. I have now told all I have to tell — I entirely acquit my old comrade, and I must beg you to withdraw the accusation against him.'

After having thus spoken, Jörgen laid himself down in his bed, closed his eyes, and seemed to take no further notice of what was going on around him. Neither did he seem to notice Ebbe, who stole softly towards his bed, seized his hand, and carried it to his lips.

The smith was very angry, and repeated and maintained his version of the affair, with gesticulations, oaths, and asseverations, in his strange lingo. He could not understand why Jörgen exercised such generous forbearance: the judge, on the contrary, comprehended it all; he called Ebbe into the other room, and had a long communication with him; after which he broke up the meeting, dismissed the witnesses, and left the cottage himself. Jörgen and Ebbe were the only persons who remained in it.

Some time elapsed, during which both remained perfectly silent. At length Jörgen raised himself in his bed, and asked,

'Are they gone?'

'Yes.'

'Every one of them?'

'Yes, we are alone.'

'Sit down by my bed, Ebbe; I have something to say to you.'

Ebbe obeyed. At that moment his whole appearance evinced the utmost humility; he did not dare to raise his eyes before Jörgen, who contemplated him calmly, but with a penetrating look.

'What I said a little while ago,' began Jörgen, 'was to save you, and because I could not live under the idea that I had another man's misfortune on my conscience. You are now free—acquitted—and no one can do anything to you. With God's blessing, I may also become well again, and recover my strength so as to be able to work as formerly; but you must yourself perceive, Ebbe, that we two can never more live and labour together. That Saturday night has rendered it necessary for us to separate for ever. I can never banish it from my memory. You shed tears now, indeed, and are deeply afflicted. I also have shed many tears when I reflected that it was you, my only companion and comrade, that had the heart to deal with me as you did.` In Heaven's name, then, let each of us go his own way. The world is surely large enough for us both. When I am stronger, and able to work, I will pay you for the part you own in this cottage and in the boat; for I hardly think you will like to remain longer here. In fact, I think it would be better for you to seek some other place to settle yourself, where people could not say anything against you. You cannot fail to perceive that the smith does not believe the declaration I made to the judge. He will tell the story his way in the town yonder, and that won't be in your favour. As I have said, when I am better you shall receive the share that belongs to you of what we have hitherto held in partnership, and we must separate.'

'Then you have found the treasure?' asked Ebbe, hurriedly.

'No,' said Jörgen, gravely. 'But the smith has promised to let me marry his daughter, and he will advance me the money to pay you.'

'I do not care about the money,' replied Ebbe; 'you are welcome to keep it all.'

'Oh yes—so you say *now*,' answered Jörgen; 'but you would repent that offer to-morrow. No, let the arrangement I have proposed stand. And you had better go, Ebbe, before the smith returns. You know that he is very passionate, and you might get into a quarrel with him. Besides, I am weak and weary, and must get some sleep. Farewell, and may the Almighty bestow on you kinder feelings towards those among whom you may henceforth seek to win your bread, than you have shown to me. Shake hands with me, Ebbe, and then go.'

Jörgen sank back on his bed, and Ebbe left the cottage.

The following five years brought about a striking difference between the fates of the two fishermen. Jörgen had married the smith's daughter. He gave up fishing, sold his boat and established himself in the little town of Væderso. There he betook himself to husbandry: he tilled the ground, ploughed, sowed, planted; in short he laboured with all the indefatigable activity, energy, and diligence, for which the inhabitants of the west country are so celebrated. At the end of two years he sold his house to buy a larger one on a thriving farm; field after field was added, and all prospered with him. Success seemed to smile on everything he undertook from the period that he relinquished his partnership with Ebbe.

'You have got an excellent son-in-law, smith,' said the peasants to Harfiz, often when they came to his smithy.

'He gets on very well,' the learned smith would reply, with a cheerful nod, indicative of content. 'But let me tell you, and you may believe what I say, that it was my medicine which has made him what he is. He has been quite another sort of man since I cured him, and restored him, I may say, to life, after Ebbe had killed him. He will be a greater man still.'

The prophecy was fulfilled as time passed on; for every year that went over his head brought some addition to Jörgen's prosperity. He was a happy man in his own family, and in all his transactions he was clever, prudent, and far-seeing.

The same space of time that seemed to have had wings for Jörgen, had crawled on slowly, unprofitably, and wearily for Ebbe. A portion of the sum he had received for his share of the cottage and the boat was appropriated to the purchase of the little plot of ground near Oxby church, where the mate had said his treasure was buried. The acquisition was not an expensive one certainly, for at that period a large quantity of waste land could be bought for about two dollars; so that after Ebbe had become the proprietor of the place, he had sufficient money left to build a house for himself on a corner of the ground he had bought.

Then commenced a course of labour which, in exertion, perseverance, and endurance, was far beyond anything Jörgen ever attempted, and yet was productive of no good results. The three stones were taken up and thrown aside, in order not to obstruct the work; then the elder-tree was removed; and after every obstacle had disappeared, Ebbe dug down, and down, until he came to the stratum of iron-hard, solid rock, which is to be found in that part of the country.

His labours were carried on by night, and with the utmost secrecy, not to attract attention. During the day he rested, and either spent the hours lounging by the sea-side, or he slept. But, whether waking or sleeping, he was haunted by the thoughts of the hidden treasure, and of the wealth he would acquire, and the consequence he would attain, when he discovered and enjoyed it. It was shocking to see that pale and meagre creature, when the moon shone upon the scene of his labours, working away eagerly, bending over the spade, and listening anxiously when every fresh heap of earth was cast up: by turns cheating himself with hopes of success, then groaning at his disappointment, yet still persevering in the search for a prize which continued to evade his grasp.

In winter the ground was frozen, and as Ebbe was obliged to cease his digging, he left his hut, and went to Hjerting, where he hired himself out among the peasantry as a day-labourer. His history soon oozed out, and his very shy, reserved manners prevented him from making acquaintances, while his fellow-labourers jeered him. 'There goes the gold-digger!' the children would cry after him when he showed himself in the streets. These scoffers, who beheld him now in so humble a position, by-and-by, when he had found the treasure, should witness his triumph. 'Wait a little!' he thought; 'success will come at last, and the day cannot be very far distant!'

When spring succeeded to winter, Ebbe left the service he had taken, and returned to his hut, where he recommenced his labours with as much assiduity as before, and with the same result. The small space in which his operations were carried on soon resembled a deep pit, wherein gravel and sand, stone and clay, were gathered together in large heaps. But the treasure was nowhere visible.

When at length the ground had been entirely turned up, every inch examined, and he could dig no lower down, Ebbe fell into the deepest despair; his last hope had vanished, and with it all the strength and energy which hope alone had sustained.

He was found one day sitting on the outside of the door of his hut, gazing on vacancy straight before him, lost in a reverie from which nothing seemed to have the power of rousing him.

At this very time a report was spread in the neighbourhood that Jörgen and his father-in-law had found *the shipwrecked mariner's treasure*—for this appeared the easiest mode of accounting for the increasing prosperity of the heretofore young fisherman. Ebbe heard this rumour; he believed it, and this belief added greatly to the bitterness of his disappointment, and was as poison to his mind.

Three years afterwards, a wan, wasted, spectral-looking figure might be seen wandering about in the vicinity of Hjerting: it was the unfortunate Ebbe, who had become deranged. The harmless lunatic was received into the poor-house at Hjerting, but spent most of his days in a remote and secluded valley, away among the sand hills. There he might be heard singing and talking to himself, whilst he occupied himself diligently in digging deep holes in the sand. One winter evening he did not return, as usual, to the poor-house. The next morning he was found, frozen to death, in a grave—it might be called —which he had dug in the sand the day before.

DAMON AND PYTHIAS.

FROM THE DANISH OF CARL BERNHARD.

In the so-called good old times, when grown-up people could sometimes be childish—now-a-days even children themselves are above such infirmities—in these good old times one often heard a ballad, a favourite song, which was as common as the lively popular airs that are now repeated nightly at the casinos; but these old songs were by no means lively, for lively music was not then in vogue; the songs were almost all sentimental. There was one ditty about 'Friendship, Hope, and Love,' in which Love was depicted as 'light red,' and of which I can now remember but two lines. It was very generally sung:

> 'Friendship rarely doth abound.
> Tell me where it can be found!'

Yes, where can it be found? All mankind seek for it; everyone wishes to have a friend. Most people believe, for a time, that they have found one; but when the friendship comes to be tested, it disappears, and they discover their mistake. Why does it disappear? Who knows why? But that it does most frequently disappear is quite certain.

Formerly, even in the grey olden times, long before anybody thought about friendship being violated, they must have had hard work enough to find the genuine article, else there would not surely have been such a fuss made about the three classical pairs of friends whose names we have all learned by heart —Damon and Pythias, Orestes and Pylades, Euryalus and Nisus—all of whom were never distinguished for anything, as far as I have been able to discover, except that they lived as friends, and ultimately died as friends.

It is surprising enough that, whilst everyone understands the words *a friend* in a good sense, there should be some little hesitation about the exact meaning of *a good friend*, and that the more eulogizing and confirmatory adjectives are added to it, the less respect it should inspire, until *a real good old friend* has become almost synonymous with a stupid old blockhead, or a cunning old rogue. If one were only to hear the following disjointed words of a conversation, 'Oh, yes, he is a good friend enough,' nine out of ten would indubitably fancy that the speakers were alluding to some matter in which one party had been taken in, and would think that what had happened manifested the credulity of that saying, in which all the ten firmly believe, 'Save me from my friends, and I will save myself from my enemies!' Undeniably, there is some truth in this sentence, and however little there may be, it is sad that one must admit there is any at all.

One of my—but I may be misconstrued myself if I say one of my good friends; I shall therefore, for the present, confine myself to calling him a worthy acquaintance of mine—had, from his earliest childhood, been an enthusiastic worshipper of friendship. Nothing more natural, for friendship is so inherent a feeling in the breast of every human being, of either sex, that it is a desire of the soul, which it strives to realize even before it thinks of love. His predilection for friendship was, it may be said, born with him, as people may be born with a propensity for stealing or drunkenness; and when he was not more than four years of age, and his grown-up relatives would have it that his little cousin should be his 'little wife'—for big people are always too ready to begin putting nonsense into the heads of children, he used to get angry, and declare that she should not be his wife, but his friend.

And when he had grown older, and had commenced his classical studies, he raved about being a Damon to some Pythias. He was an excellent lad, cheerful, good-natured, good-looking, and by no means deficient in talent; in short, he was in all respects a steady schoolboy, but perhaps he carried a little too far his ideas about friendship. He had not, however, then attached himself to any one individual among his companions; he was on good terms with them all, while he thirsted after one, only *one* true friend, as a celebrated author is known to have wished but one reader, but that one to be capable of understanding him thoroughly.

I withhold his name, for he is now in so conspicuous a station that many of my readers must know him, and it would, perhaps, annoy him to see his name in print, for he is one of those folks who have an old-fashioned dislike to what they call 'appearing in print;' that is to say, being named publicly. I shall designate him by one of his first names, which he used in his boyish years—*viz*. Mikkel; it is an ugly name, but he is not to blame for that, since his opinion about it was not asked. When he was christened, his parents had called him after a rich old uncle, who, the good people thought, might, on that account, at a future day, leave him a large legacy. It is a bad custom to make innocent children suffer for their parents' bad taste in choosing names, and to inflict on them ill-sounding family names, either because these had been chosen by a generation who had queer notions, or from selfishness and from speculation, as in the case in question. Mikkel was grown up, and had undergone much jeering on account of his frightful name, but his uncle did not leave him a stiver! It was a shameful trick—a positive fraud, the parents naturally thought. No one can blame Mikkel because he would no longer put up with the disagreeable appellation, especially as it had come to his ears that a young girl had given her suitor a basket solely on account of his name. She said, 'he had such a shockingly ugly name, that she never could bring herself to say, my sweet Morten. Dear no! the sound made her shudder, and one really must be able to say *sweet* to one's lover.' Morten and Mikkel are much on a par. He renounced, therefore, the name of the ungrateful uncle, and selected for the future one of the high-sounding names which had also been bestowed on him at his baptism, like that shoemaker's son who was christened Jens Napoleon Petersen. Nevertheless, I should prefer to call him Damon, that savouring more of the anonymous, and this I will do with the permission of my kind readers.

When he and I went to school together, we got on very well, and were on good terms; but no sworn and patented friendship took place between us. It happened one day, as we were walking together outside of one of the gates of the town, on a Friday, and he was lost in his Damon-Pythias dreams, which went in at one of my ears and out at the other, we met a school companion, who was crying as he came out of a house. The good-hearted Damon stopped him, and asked what was the cause of his distress, and we were informed that our comrade had been visiting *a good friend*. Damon could not see that there was any cause for howling about this; he would have been glad enough to have been in his place. Yes, but our unlucky school companion had received a sound drubbing from his good friend, and from some of the latter's good friends, because he would not be always their horse, and drag them in the little carriage; he wished to take his turn to go inside of it, at least for once, but they abused him like a pickpocket, and beat him; this was always the way he was served, and it was a great shame, for he had liked his friend so much; but now he would have nothing more to do with him. And when he had told him that he was going to break with him, the fellow had thumped him well, and turned him out of doors, and it was almost dinner-time, and now he had no friend—and he would get no dinner!

The soft-hearted Damon offered him forthwith his friendship and a dinner; the boy went home with him to his parents' house, where he dined, and immediately afterwards staunch brotherhood was sworn, and the empty place in Damon's heart was filled up! Fate had granted his wish, and he had providentially found a friend!

Mikkel was a happy boy; he had now truly become Damon, and the other was Pythias. It was a strong friendship, whose not few thorns seemed to Damon like so many roses. He had to thrash his companion's former friend, and fight all that friend's chums, in order to revenge his Pythias, and prove their misconduct to him; and he got many a bruise, and many a torn jacket in these battles, which merged into a long, lasting war — a war he had to sustain alone, for Pythias stood aloof. He had to write all his friend's exercises, and prompt him every day in his lessons, which Pythias, trusting to Damon's friendship, had neglected to learn, and this cost the latter many a scold from the master, who had observed it. But if ever he happened to require the least help himself, he got none, for Pythias was incapable of giving it. Damon not only shared all the nice things he had with his friend, but he often gave him the largest portion, and, indeed, sometimes the whole; but he never got anything in return. Pythias took care to eat all his good things by himself; but Damon never dreamed of finding fault with this; he was pleased and proud of being able to make various useful presents to his friend, and loved him the better for it. Thus passed the whole of his school-days; and in consequence of this sworn friendship the two were called by all the boys Damon and Pythias.

They were at length to separate, and each to go his own way. 'I am sorry I am obliged to part with you, I shall miss you very much,' said Pythias, when the farewell moment came.

'I don't know how I shall exist without you,' said Damon. 'I am truly wretched!'

They agreed to write to each other often. Damon

did write letter after letter, but never received an answer; that grieved him extremely. He was taken ill about six months afterwards, but I will not say that it was disappointed friendship that made him ill; he had caught an epidemic which was raging then, and had a long illness. Though Pythias knew this, he had never once inquired for his school friend. As soon as he could hold a pen, Damon wrote to him over and over again—no reply! Then he buried his friendship in his silent, faithful breast, until at last it died, long after it had been buried.

His student-days arrived, and found him full of the enthusiasm of youth. Damon longed for all that was beautiful and noble, but especially for friendship. Love had not yet touched him. I believe that he looked upon it as a sickly, unmanly feeling, which could not be indulged in without relinquishing the energy and the strength of mind that ought to characterize a man! Poor Damon! I verily believe such was his opinion.

Well, Damon found at length his Pythias; but not the old Pythias, for whom he had toiled and fought, and who had repaid him with such ingratitude. No; a bran new Pythias had he stumbled upon, one who, like himself, was 'a master in the kingdom of mind ;' one who like himself, was devoted to the true and the beautiful ; one who, he thought, could sympathize with him in everything, and to whom he attached himself with the strongest ties of friendship—a really good friend.

And this friendship lasted for some years—during the whole time they were at the university—and they were nicknamed Damon and Pythias, to the great satisfaction of one of the friends at least. Damon was certainly a kind and trustworthy friend. He wrote with untiring patience all the tedious college manuscripts; Pythias used them almost always, and, moreover, lent them to strangers, so that Damon never could get them when he wanted them himself. Damon bought all the books they both required, for Pythias needed his own money for other purposes ; and when Pythias wanted them no longer he sold them. Damon remained at home from balls, that Pythias might borrow his dress-coat, as he did not think his own good enough; and Damon rejoiced that he had a good coat which fitted Pythias so well. Not a week passed that Pythias did not borrow money from Damon, of which he never made any memorandum. Pythias was fond of going to the theatre, and he always went to the boxes.

One day, when Damon suggested that it would be better for him to go to the pit with him, for the money which one box ticket cost would pay two pit tickets, and they might go there and amuse themselves together, as he really could not afford the more expensive places, Pythias replied that he by no means wished his friend to spend his money in going to the theatre on his account, that he only wanted *to borrow* the money for his own ticket, as he was out of cash at the moment, but he could not think of going to such a place as the pit. And the good-natured Damon gave him the last shilling he had, and remained at home, rejoicing that his dear friend was amusing himself in the boxes.

At length they were both to graduate, and Pythias held his ground only because Damon had been an unwearied grinder for him, and had devoted himself, early and late, to cramming him in order to pull him through. His success delighted Damon much more than his own.

There was some talk of a foreign tour—and they were both candidates for the stipend accorded for that purpose — what a pleasure if they could travel together! But this year there was only *one* stipend to be given away; Damon was sure of getting it, having been the cleverest student. Pythias adjured him, of course in the name of friendship, to resign his claim, because, for many important reasons, it was necessary for him—Pythias—to get away for a time; in fact, he could hold out no longer, while Damon had many other resources. Damon pondered on the subject, but could not find out what these resources were; nevertheless, he withdrew his petition, and left the field open to Pythias, but he endeavoured in vain, also in friendship's name, to induce him to confide to him the important reasons which had influenced his dear Pythias to demand the sacrifice he had made for him. He was enlightened as to the truth, however, afterwards. When Pythias had obtained the stipend, and was off, it came out that he had been, for a long time, in the habit of gambling, and that he had lost a great deal at play. The debts he had left he transferred to his friend in an affected, high-flown, bombastic epistle to his 'dear, faithful Damon,' and in order that the latter, to whom he bade farewell for ever, might still more highly honour friendship, he had drawn without asking leave a few little bills of exchange in his name, wherein his writing was so cleverly imitated, that Damon himself had the utmost difficulty in distinguishing it from his own!

To one who had for so many years put entire confidence in the reciprocity of the ardent and sincere friendship he himself had felt, it was a severe blow to meet such scandalous treachery. Damo took measures to have the bills of exchange paid, and, with a bleeding heart, he buried Pythias the Second!

Damon now forswore friendship, and withdrew himself from society; it was easy to do this, for his circle had been principally composed of Pythias's acquaintances, and he did not much relish seeing them now—he did not like to hear them pulling Pythias to pieces, and recounting the many dirty tricks he had played them, to whom he had also pretended to have been a good friend. Damon commenced his professional career, and found comfort in his occupations; but his heart was lonely.

One evening he read in the work of a celebrated philosopher the following sentence:

'The dog is man's best friend—it alone is faithful.'

These words made a deep impression on him. Within eight days he had purchased a dog, a large handsome Newfoundlander, of a good breed. It was then only in its puppy years, and had to be brought up to obedience and cleanliness; this cost him the trouble of bestowing sundry good thrashings on the animal, but Damon knew that he who loves the child spares not the rod, and he loved his dog as if it had been his child, until it should be educated to become his friend. Hector would receive his caning, steal up to his master's feet, lick his hand, sigh deeply, and at the slightest glance of encouragement would spring up joyfully and wag his tail. When Damon looked up from his employment, he always encountered Hector's friendly gaze. When he took his hat and stick, the dog would start up from his place near the stove, if he were even in the soundest sleep, to follow him through thick and thin, by day or by-night. Truly, the philosopher was right; the dog is man's faithful friend, and Hector was not troublesome, and he obeyed no other being in this world but his master— they were friends.

This friendship lasted for a couple of years, and it filled up in a certain degree the vacancy in Damon's heart, and cheered his lonely hours.

But gradually this friendship took the same turn

as love often does—the one loves, and the other allows himself or herself to be loved. The parts they played changed gradually; Damon assumed the dog's part, and became humble, obedient, and faithful, whilst Hector took the master's part, and turned capricious, tyrannical, and ungrateful. The four-footed creature had become almost like a man, from being the constant companion of his two-legged friend. Damon put up with all this, and the dog imposed upon him in his canine fashion, exactly as the schoolboy and the student had imposed on him formerly in their human fashion.

Damon had had many disagreeables to encounter latterly. One day he came home very much fretted, with his head full of some tiresome business papers, which absolutely required his immediate attention. He patted his favourite, spoke to him as to a friend who could understand him, complained to Hector of the provoking chief of the department who had annoyed him, and Hector fixed on him a thoughtful look; it was as if the dog comprehended how hard it is to be annoyed. This did his heart good; he recovered his spirits, and began to work away vigorously at the papers he had brought home with him. But Hector got angry at finding himself neglected, and also he wanted to go out to walk. 'No, my friend, it is impossible—don't disturb me —down, down—there is no time for walking just now!' The dog became importunate, and was patted, and dismissed; he then became obstinate, and laid his clumsy paw upon the table, so that the inkstand was upset over the numerous half-finished papers. For that he got a slap; he became enraged, and tried to drag his master off of his chair; Damon kicked him away, expecting that he would then be quiet, but it made him worse, and he rushed upon him. Damon also got angry; he seized the ruler, and struck Hector with it, who, however, dragged the chair from under him with his teeth and paws. The one swore, the other growled; it was, certes, anything but friendship that was displayed in this scene, which collected all the inhabitants of the house on the outside of Damon's door, in terror at this unusual dog-fight.

I arrived at that moment, having come to speak to Damon on some business. It was an awful plight in which I found him: excited, bitten, and with his clothes torn; whilst the dog stood snarling over the broken chair, with a brutal, triumphant look, flashing eyes, and teeth set. It was evident that he knew he was the master there, and he looked with anything but a friendly expression at the subdued Damon.

'And this illusion has fled also!' he said to me, when we had taken up the overturned chair, and gathered together the scattered and ink-stained papers.

'And thou also, Brutus!' he exclaimed with a comical degree of gravity, and a melancholy glance at the sullen-looking dog.

'The bestia bruta!' said I. 'This comes of choosing four-footed friends.' And I seized the opportunity of bestowing upon him a lecture about his animal mania, which had made him quite an oddity, and had withdrawn him from the society of rational beings. Shame, suffering, and anger brought him over to my way of thinking; he made a threatening gesture towards Hector, who instantly rose up and showed his teeth; he was evidently ready to renew the battle at any moment. It was really too absurd.

After a great deal of persuasion, I prevailed on Damon to go home with me, and conclude that uncomfortable evening among my family circle. Before we left his lodgings, I privately requested the landlord to have Hector removed to an inn, where he could be tied up till the next day, when I should come to say what was to be done with him.

The evening passed off tolerably well; it succeeded in dissipating his chagrin. I accompanied him home towards midnight, and before I left him I had obtained his permission to send Hector into the country, to a relation of mine, where he would be well treated and be useful as a chained dog, for Damon himself perceived that he could not be made a friend of, and that he was too ill-tempered and dangerous to be allowed to go about loose. And thus was Pythias the Third, the four-footed, deposed.

It was very strange that though he wanted sadly to have his Pythias's place refilled, he never made the slightest overture to me to occupy it. Nevertheless, we were very intimate. He often visited me, and found pleasure in the society of my family, and more especially in that of a young girl, who was a frequent guest at my house, and who was both pretty and good, though, perhaps, being a country girl, she wanted a little of that finer polish which can only be acquired in the capital.

I have no doubt it was her being so open, straightforward, unsophisticated, and natural, that charmed him with her; oddly enough, love was never mentioned by either of them; they always spoke of friendship alone, up to the very day of their betrothal. And, indeed, after they were betrothed there was no change in their manners to each other. I never saw him show her any of the usual little attentions, or bestow on her any of the little endearments so common during this period; he always spoke to her as if she had been a male friend; it seemed as if he could not perceive that she belonged to womankind.

This engagement delighted us all, especially my sensible wife, who augured a peaceful future for them, a life devoid of passion's storms, calm and even, and rendered comfortable by a competence sufficient for all their wants, though it could not be called a fortune, according to the common acceptation of the word.

The damsel's parents gladly gave their consent, and as Damon very justly considered a long engagement a wearisome affair, before six months had passed they were man and wife.

The young girl was certainly a sweet pretty bride, and I really cannot imagine how Damon could be satisfied with calling her 'my friend,' as he led her from the altar; and I was still more surprised next day to find that she had already begun to look after her household matters. There was nothing to be found fault with in this, to be sure, and neither of them seemed to think this out of the usual way. The young couple appeared to be quite happy, and it was to be supposed that Damon's heart had at last found its haven of rest. He had his young wife, all went as she wished, and his house was, therefore, a pleasant one; it was evident that it was under the care of a good and kind spirit.

I have observed that there is one thing which is a stumbling-block in almost all young *ménages*— that is, the continued intimacy, after marriage, of the husband's young men friends. Most young wives seem to think that they must keep a watchful eye upon these friends, and quietly strive to put an end to their baneful influence over the husband! for they suppose that these former companions will withdraw his thoughts from the sanctity of domestic life and lead him into naughty ways. These suspicions seem to be deeply rooted in the minds of newly-married women. I sincerely believe they are suggested by young wives, who ought to know better by experience, and might have perceived that their husbands' earlier associates would, in general, be glad to be received as members of the family circle. The wives imagine that their dominion is insecure so long as these suspicious persons are on board; they think that when such is the case the ship of matrimony may be at any moment upset, or stranded on unknown shores, that they must steer with a skilful hand, and that they cannot be safe until they have had the husbands' early friends cast overboard. I can assert this from experience, for I have myself been cast overboard more than once on account of such groundless suspicions.

But a house can hardly be without visitors, and what is more natural than that these should consist of the young wife's friends and connections? She believes she can depend upon them; she is accustomed to them; she likes to display to them her notable housekeeping; it is so very natural, and therefore one generally sees the husband's friends and relations by degrees supplanted by those of the wife.

Damon's wife, however, was not obliged to manœuvre at all to get rid of his especial friends, for, with the exception of myself, who had my own house, and was already a sedate and discreet person, he never invited a single old associate. It was not necessary for her to throw anyone overboard to make room for her friends and relations; these were self-elected intimates at Mikkel's house, and all went on well there.

There was one of her cousins in particular to whom Damon soon attached himself. He was a young man who had exactly the qualities which were wanting in Damon. He was, among other things, witty, lively, amusing; he was at all times ready for anything, and knew how to make the best of everything. Damon soon found that he could not do without him, and he became a daily guest at his house, which there was nothing in the way of business to prevent his being, as he lived in a state of *il dolce far niente*, waiting until some good appointment might offer itself, which might suit a person of his talents and pretensions.

Before the expiration of a year, I observed that by degrees a change had taken place in their relative positions. Damon had by this time nearly undermined his own happiness. His old Pythias folly had awoke again in him, almost without his being conscious of it. His interest in his young wife was actually cast into the shade by his friendship for her cousin, who had become Pythias the Fourth. She discovered at length that she was quite set aside, and was jealous of this neglect; at the same time she grew more and more intimate with her cousin, whose lively conversation pleased her. That he had fallen in love with his young cousin I will not assert, but he paid her at times such marked attention, that I often thought this was the only reasonable inference to be drawn from his conduct; at other times there was so much levity and carelessness in his manners, so much flightiness in his way of talking, that I felt myself compelled to discard the supposition. Certain it is, however, that he was always hovering around her; that her reputation might run the risk of being injured by his demeanour towards her, and that dangerous consequences really might arise from their being so much together in the intimacy of daily life, yet—who was to blame except Damon?

With his accustomed blindness, the husband could not see anything of this; he made quite sure that it was entirely for *his* sake that the young man played chess, talked politics, smoked tobacco, and went out to walk or to fish whenever Damon wished to go. In order that they might manage to be still more together, he had prevailed upon the cousin to come out and stay with him at a country-house he had hired at a few miles from town, where they had plenty of room. This invitation was given much against the wishes of his wife, who had tried to prevent it, but she had consented to it when she found that Damon had set his heart on it. He said, jestingly, that he could not do without some male society, and a trio would be pleasant in their pastoral life. In this trio he himself voluntarily assigned the second part to the cousin, while he took the third to himself.

Damon, however, was a little changed; he felt no longer inclined to be *quite* so subservient in his friendship as he had formerly been with his two- and his four-footed friends. By degrees, a desire had crept into his mind to take his revenge, and for once become himself the domineering party. He began to be somewhat importunate in his claims on the time and companionship of the cousin, who, on his side, showed decided symptoms of wishing to emancipate himself, especially from the tiresome and frequent fishing expeditions to the neighbouring lake; but fishing was perhaps Damon's greatest pleasure, especially when he had the company of a good friend. Damon was annoyed that the cousin had several times latterly excused himself from accompanying him, and, not caring to go alone, he had been obliged to relinquish his favourite amusement. One day—it was too bad—on a beautiful evening in the very height of summer, he refused to go fishing, when there could be no earthly reason for his doing so—none that Damon could discover, except that he preferred to parade up and down the alley of linden-trees at the other end of the garden with his wife—while he himself sat at the top of the stone stairs, and fretted until he was quite out of humour. He could see that they spoke eagerly to each other, and laughed, and amused themselves, while he was wearying himself; and neither of them seemed to be thinking of him or his *ennui*. What were they going to do now? So! They were actually setting off to walk in the very direction of the lake, where he would so gladly have gone to fish; but *then*, it was too far to go, forsooth!—now, they could go notwithstanding the distance. It was almost like defying him; that was probably the cousin's intention.

A disagreeable light seemed to dawn on his mind.

And when this operation first begins to take place, a man is apt to fancy more than he has valid grounds for supposing. And this was the case with Damon.

In an exceedingly unpleasant state of mind, he returned to the usual sitting-room in search of some employment to make time pass less heavily. The comfortable room spoke volumes to his excited mind, with its quiet and peace. It was arranged by his wife's taste, everything bore witness in her favour. There stood her work-table, there lay her work, the half-finished embroidery which she was preparing for his birthday, and at which he therefore avoided looking. Upon a table close by hers lay the cousin's portfolios and drawing materials. There was no necessity for the tables being so near each other, and he pushed the table with the drawings a little way from the work-table. The young man certainly had talent — there were comical sketches and little landscapes, thrown off as illustrations of poems, not without genius; he thought he would just look into the portfolios, when, in opening one of them, a sheet of paper, with pencil drawings, slipped out of it. What were these? He must see. They were a whole row of caricatures, in doing which the cousin excelled. There was a man with his nightcap on, evidently asleep and snoring; a man with a pipe in his mouth, half-asleep over a fishing-rod; a man half-asleep over a chess-board; a man half-asleep over a Berlin newspaper; and lastly, a man half asleep over his tobacco-pipe, while his pretty young wife seemed dreaming over the work she had in her hand. Of what was *she* dreaming while *he* was dozing? This question forced itself upon him. The sleepy-headed man was no other than himself, caricatured in the most laughable manner; the young wife might have been taken from nature: it was a charming likeness. Damon sat as if he had fallen from the skies, with the sheet of paper in his hand; he could scarcely conceive the ingratitude which had suggested these sketches, or the barefaced impudence of leaving them in an open portfolio, in his own daily sitting-room, where anyone might see them—not only himself and his wife, but his guests and his servants also.

Fate brought me to him for a second time at a critical moment. I came accidentally to pay him a visit, and found him somewhat in the same state as on the evening Hector had been doing battle with him. I entered into his angry feelings, but nevertheless could hardly refrain from bursting into a fit of laughter at the exceedingly impertinent, but very droll drawings. We had a serious conversation on the position in which he was placed; with great difficulty I brought him, at length, to perceive that much of the blame rested with himself, and that his young wife had nothing to reproach herself with. I combated his assertion that she must have been cognizant of the existence of these caricatures, and must have sat for the likeness of herself; and I even went so far as to promise to prove to him her ignorance of the drawings, though I did not know how that was to be effected without occasioning a *scene*—and I had the greatest horror of scenes.

We had a long conversation, we two, for the wife and the cousin remained a good while absent—longer than I thought was exactly right, especially as it was getting late; but Damon did not seem to think about it; he was engaged in speculating on the theme I had suggested for his consideration—namely, that a husband who never makes the slightest effort to find amusement for his young wife, but, without the least compunction, leaves her to solitude or weariness, has himself to blame if another succeeds in interesting and amusing her. It is this unfortunate transition from the devoted assiduity of the days of courtship, to the sleepy security of married life, that so often undermines love, and renders the heart empty; and nature has decreed that a woman's heart can never remain long perfectly vacant.

At last the truants returned. It was evident that the lady, at least, felt it was not quite right to have stayed out till so long after the usual hour for tea; she bustled about to get the tea ready, and was very attentive in helping us to it. Damon maintained a grave silence, and I felt somewhat embarrassed; the cousin alone seemed quite at his ease, and not at all *gêné;* I could not make out whether this was nature or art. Perhaps it was politic to appear as if he had no idea that there could be any cause for animadversion on account of their unusually long walk. My confidence in her began to waver a little, whilst my anger at him increased.

After tea the conversation fell, b ymere accident, on portrait painting. It was the lady who brought the subject forward, by speaking of a picture of a female which she had observed in passing, hanging like a sign, over the open door of a garden. Nothing could have been more *à propos*. I hastened to ask the young wife if she had ever had her likeness taken. No, she never had, and she never intended to have it taken, for she could not bear the idea that anyone should sit down and stare at her. The cousin declared this was a silly objection, and appealed to me if he were not right.

'Oh! that is because he wants to make a sketch of me himself,' she said, in rather a hurried manner; 'he has often begged me to permit it, but I won't do so.'

The cousin remarked that there was no question of permission, only of complaisance; if he chose to make a portrait of her, he could do it without asking her leave; he could take her likeness without her knowing anything about it; he could do it from memory. His cousin laughed at these assertions, and laughed so naturally, that I felt quite convinced I was right about her. Damon, on the contrary, looked more and more distressed as this conversation proceeded; it was quite apparent to me that he was miserable, and in a painful state of doubt, and I had promised him a proof of his wife's innocence. Without uttering a word, I laid hold of a corner of the paper on which were the treacherous drawings, drew it out of the portfolio, and handed it to her. I admit that this was very hard on the cousin, but why should

I spare the young jackanapes, from whom no mercy for others was to be expected, as his caricatures showed plainly enough?

She evidently did not know what I meant by showing the drawings to her, or what she was to do with them. On the first glance at the paper, she seemed about to burst into a fit of laughter, and no one who had seen these capital caricatures of Damon could have blamed the child of nature for doing so. But on the second look, her eye had had time to run over the whole sheet, and she had beheld her own likeness; the contrast was too glaring, and there now did not linger the slightest trace of a smile on her countenance. She blushed crimson, threw the sketches far away from her, as if they had burned her hand, which for a short time she placed over her eyes, as one does when suddenly coming to the brink of a precipice. And her womanly tact had assuredly told her that such had been her position. It was a moment for a painter of scenes from domestic life to have taken a sketch. In the background were the open doors leading from the pretty sitting-room to the garden, whose trees seemed drawn on the clear evening skies in their full beauty. On the sofa sat a man, apparently very unhappy, with his cheek resting on his hand, and a look expressive of the deepest anxiety fixed upon a young woman, whose guiltless countenance rivalled the glow of the evening sky; whose whole bearing evinced mingled anger and humility, innocence and embarrassment, while her eyes were riveted on the paper she had cast from her, which had revealed to her one of the dark shades of life. At a little distance from her stood a grave-looking man, whose face expressed perfect confidence in, and esteem for, the young wife; he stood as if he wished to inspire her with courage to follow the dictates of her own heart. And nearest the door leading to the entrance-hall sat a young gentleman, whose assured, careless deportment formed a strong contrast to his perplexed and irresolute glances; no one could have doubted that he was the cause of the dismal mood which had seized upon all the rest of the party, and that he was aware of this himself.

But it was only for a few short moments that the young wife stood as described. Presently she looked up fearlessly, although tears were streaming down her cheeks; without vouchsafing a single glance to the young gentleman, she swept past him, threw her arms round her husband's neck, and sank, weeping, by his side on the sofa. And this charming, natural act found a response in his heart; he flung his arm round her waist, and pressed her to his breast. It was a dumb and yet an eloquent scene!

The friend and the cousin were now *de trop*. I made a sign to him, and he left the room with me, without the others appearing to notice our departure.

It was rather an embarrassing situation in which we two found ourselves placed as we walked along the high road together. But as I have always considered that 'honesty is the best policy,' I did not, on this occasion, depart from my general rule. I began by telling him frankly that the ingratitude which he had displayed towards my friend, who was also his friend, and his cousin's husband, by caricaturing him so ill-naturedly, and his hardihood in leaving the drawings in an open portfolio in a sitting-room common to all the family, as if he wished them to be seen by at least *one* member of it, had convinced me that his remaining in that house would be productive of unhappiness to his host, and would be disagreeable to all parties. It was Damon himself who by accident had found the caricatures. It was impossible, of course, that he could pass them over in silence, and their discovery might have caused an extremely unpleasant scene. I had sought to avoid this, as I knew that no explanation or apology could have been accepted; in fact, none satisfactorily could have been offered. I pointed out to the young man that it was not likely his intercourse with the family could be renewed; that it would be necessary for him to determine what he was to do with himself for the future, as he could no longer reckon on their kindness.

'Soft and fair goes far,' says the proverb, and its truth was shown here. My words were taken in good part; the cousin and I continued to walk back and forwards on the high road half the night. He accompanied me at length to town, and then there was nothing for it—if he were to have a roof over his head at all—but to give him a bed at my house. We laid our heads together to think of what could be done to procure a situation for him, which might give him some profitable employment for the present, and some prospect of advantage for the future; and at last we both agreed that he had better look after an appointment in one of the provincial towns, which had just become vacant, and in the disposal of which I had some influence. Security, however, to a certain small extent, would be required, but I would help him to obtain this. I was quite certain, I said, that if I asked Damon, he would be his security, for he had a most amiable and forgiving temper. I wished Damon to have this satisfaction, and the cousin this humiliation; *that* should be his only punishment. I am now inclined to believe, however, that he found the punishment tolerably light, and bore it with great equanimity, notwithstanding that he vapoured a great deal about obligation, mortification, contrition, &c. &c.

To cut a long story short, the plan we had hit upon that night was carried out. The cousin went to the country town and obtained the situation, Damon became his security, and was not sorry to have this little revenge upon him. And his young wife, who, through my indiscretion, found out afterwards what Damon had done, was quite overcome by her husband's generosity, and thought more of him than ever. A man is never sorry that his wife should entertain the belief that he is generous and noble-minded; that raises him much more in her estimation than if he gave her occasion for the vain satisfaction of admiring his wit. That, certainly, Damon's wife had no opportunity of doing, for he possessed neither wit nor genius, but he was a good, kind-hearted person. Their married life, which had been so nearly rendered unhappy, after the cloud above referred to had cleared off, glided on in a calm and even tenour, and nothing occurred to disturb their serenity.

But man is his own worst enemy, an old philosopher has said, and not without truth. Before twelve months had expired Damon's old whim had revived: he longed again for a friend, and began to lament that he had no one to whom he might speak on many subjects on which he could not converse with his wife.

'To speak the honest truth,' he said to me one day, 'I miss my wife's cousin exceedingly. He was a pleasant, sociable young man as could be, and I really do believe that we did him injustice—at least as far as my wife was concerned—and that she never would have troubled herself about him if he had remained in our house till doomsday. I really do miss him often.'

I opened my eyes in amazement at hearing this speech. But he was in earnest. Notwithstanding his domestic comforts, and all his previous unfortunate experience, he longed for—his phantom, his patented friend, his Pythias the Fifth! The old fixed idea was again in the ascendant! His folly almost made me ill, but it also made me very angry, and this time I did not let him off easily. I remonstrated with him on the injustice with which he had during his whole life treated me, who had always been his true friend, a fact which no one could deny, though he had scarcely considered me as such, while he had run up friendship after friendship with a set of worthless creatures. His Pythias-fancy was a positive frenzy with him, approaching to insanity. But he had never had the least idea of what friendship *really was*. And as he was ignorant of it, I would tell him that friendship is the reward of affection, and it is not to be found in the street, like acquaintances, the mere result of chance. But what had he gained by his various friendships? Had they not been for a long time a wretched slavery, and in the last instance an equally wretched attempt at governing? The absurdity had merged at length into a perfect monomania, which deserved no mercy, for it had nearly made his poor wife thoroughly unhappy. If he could not give up the indulgence of this caprice, I advised him to engage a Pythias by the month for certain stipulated wages; some poor devil whom he could order to go with him to fish, or sit down to a chessboard whenever he pleased, for he required no other companion. Such an arrangement would be very convenient, because he could dismiss the hired Pythias when he pleased without further ado. As to myself, I said, I should continue to visit at his house only on his wife's account, for, as she was to be so neglected by him, she might require in her isolation the occasional society of a sincere friend. I should not come any longer for his sake, as he had shown me plainly enough how little he cared, or had ever cared, for me.

Damon was quite dumbfounded at the warmth with which I spoke, and at the unvarnished truths with which I overwhelmed him; his conscience must have told him that my accusations were not without foundation. He gave in, and concord was restored between us upon the condition that, for the future, he should renounce all search after his Pythias puppets. It was further resolved that the pacification should be 'firm and lasting,' as it is called in all treaties of peace.

I had been two or three months travelling abroad, when I received a letter from Damon, giving me to understand that an event was expected in his house which was looked forward to with much pleasure. I was delighted to hear it, hoping that it would add so much to the happiness of my friends in the future. At length, to my joy, came another letter, announcing the birth of a son, his exact image, and he was so expansive in his descriptions of the little stranger, whom he seemed to look upon as a prodigy, that he scarcely left himself room to mention his wife.

As soon as I returned home, I went to see him, and found him, like a fond papa, in the nursery, where he was pacing up and down, holding a monologue about the boy's education and future prospects. The young mother was sitting on the sofa with that languid, touching expression of heartfelt joy, which is so becoming to young mothers, and with a dreamy look, as if she, too, were beholding in her mind's eye the future for her child, and in thought were bestowing on him the cherub form more meet for an angel than a child of mortality. I congratulated them both with all my heart. Damon lifted his 'exact image' from the cradle, raised the infant high in the air, and exclaimed with pleasure and pride :

'See here! here is my new born friend—my rightful Pythias!'

I could not help smiling at this truly unexpected outburst. What obstinacy!

The young mother held out her arms, and cried: 'Oh, give him to me—give me my child, my own little man, my darling!'

And when the infant was placed in her arms she caressed him with that tenderness which only a mother can show.

'My Pythias!—My darling!' They had both spoken from their hearts, and found the word which made them happiest.

When the boy was to be christened, the mother proposed that he should be named Charles, and the father that he should also be called Pythias. Charles was after me; Pythias was after him, the other—the phantom. I could not refrain from whispering to Damon, if it would not be well to have the child also christened 'the Fifth.' He laughed, and pushed me so, that I had nearly gone head-foremost into the cradle to 'the new-born Pythias.'

And Charles Pythias united in his own person that which makes the happiness of marriage—love and friendship. I do not believe that either of the parents bethought them how long these feelings had been shared among various individuals, so entirely were they now united and concentrated in this one little child.

But I pleaded earnestly that the boy should on no account be called Pythias, and insisted that it was quite enough for him to bear my name, as his father's friend. I was determined to free myself from hearing anything more of Pythias. Happily I carried my point, and I *did* hear no more of him. The new-born Pythias, however, took, in due time, his rightful place, though he had escaped bearing the ridiculous name.

THE FATAL CHAIN.

FROM THE SWEDISH OF UNCLE ADAM.

One dreary autumn evening, shortly after I had taken possession of my living (thus my friend, the Rev. Mr. Z., began his narrative), I was sitting alone in my study, the same which I occupy to this day, and from which I overlook the church and the churchyard, when a servant-girl entered, and announced that a strange gentleman was waiting in the drawing-room, who wished to speak to me. I hastened downstairs, and found a good-looking young man, although he appeared to be unusually pale, with an expression of wild grief in his eyes, which led me to conclude that he was the bearer of some unpleasant intelligence.

'I come to beg you for the key of the Lejonswärd'schen family vault,' said he; 'I believe you have it.'

'What!' I demanded in astonishment, 'do you wish it now, at this late hour?'

'Yes; I must have it,' said the stranger, impatiently, 'for a corpse. Alas! a corpse is to be interred immediately.'

The stranger's manners seemed to me to be so very peculiar that I still hesitated. On perceiving this he cried,

'You appear to be unwilling to give it, sir. You need not hesitate; my name is Lejonswärd, and the corpse which is to be laid in the narrow tomb is that of my wife. I have one key, but require the other from you. Will you still refuse it to me?'

I gave him the key, and with scarcely a word of thanks he hastened away. I returned to my chamber, and gazed forth into the darkness which shrouded the churchyard. I soon perceived lights moving over the graves towards the vaults; the vault lies here, on this side, and the wall at the entrance is ornamented by a lion holding in its paw a pierced heart. The tomb was opened, and I saw the torchlight through the grating. It was a gloomy sight, which I shall never forget.

The simple burial was over, and immediately afterwards a servant brought me back the key.

Several years had passed, when the same gentleman entered my room one morning.

'Do you recollect me?' he asked. I answered in the affirmative. 'It is well,' continued he; 'I am going to become your parishioner, yonder at Lejonsnäs.'

'Are you going to live at Lejonsnäs? Surely you are not in earnest, Herr Count! No one has resided there for nearly a hundred years.'

'So much the better! I will turn it once more into a human dwelling; but I shall lead a very secluded life; my servant is to be my major-domo, my coachman, and my valet; that will be a quiet household! Will you accompany me?' continued he. 'Though the proprietor of the estate, I am perfectly ignorant of its situation. Will you accompany me, and instal me among my dear forefathers who are there in effigy?'

Having acquainted my wife with my intended journey, I seated myself along with the count in his carriage, and set off, driven by the much experienced domestic, who, besides his knowledge of the mysteries of the kitchen and the bed-chamber, was also skilled in managing a pair of horses.

We soon arrived at the estate. A large, heavy building, to which wings had been added, stood, with its dingy windows, in gloomy grandeur; a double row of ancient trees skirted the spacious court-yard, in the centre of which, surrounded by a wild and partly withered hedge of box, arose a dried-up fountain. This is a slight description of the place.

The count smiled and looked at me. 'How does the house please you?' said he. 'To me it looks like the abode of spectres. It is strange,' continued he, 'that people are always anxious to attach a more intimate connection with the world of spirits to places such as this, as if spirits could not reveal their presence anywhere. You doubt my words. You shake your head. Why? If there be no communication with the world of spirits, why have we an inward voice which tells us that there is?'

'All have not such a voice,' I answered, smiling.

'There you are mistaken, dear sir,' replied the count, eagerly. 'You cannot deny that there are things which pass our comprehension, which therefore originate from a higher power; and there scarcely exists a man who, once in his life at least, has not been placed in a situation which has forced him to believe in the influence of a world of spirits. Tell me, what is it that consoles him who has lost all that he held dear? For instance, a—'—he was silent a moment, as if struggling with inward emotion—'a wife,' continued he, 'and child. What is that—when, crushed by the cruel hand of Fate, one kneels before a coffin—which illumines the soul like a clear stream of light from a better world, or whispers sweet comfort to the half-paralyzed heart?'

'Religion,' I replied; 'the consolation of religion, Herr Count.'

'No, no, Herr Pastor; religion has nothing to do with *this*. Religion is a sentiment embracing duty and devotion, which is founded on faith, and directed by reason. The sensation to which I allude is something outward, something which affects the soul as suddenly as a flash of lightning, without the thoughts having had time to dwell on the possibility of consolation. It is as if a stream of light broke unexpectedly upon the mind, Herr Pastor. It is not religion, but the spirit of the beloved departed which bestows on the mourner a portion of its own bliss.'

Just then the inspector arrived with the keys of the castle, and interrupted our conversation. He also was of the same opinion as myself, that the castle was not fit to be inhabited; but the count remained firm to his intention of taking up his abode there.

'Give me the keys, inspector. You need not accompany us; my friend and I will be able to find our way, I do not doubt. You need only tell us to which doors the keys belong.'

The inspector bowed, and began as he was requested to sort the keys.

'This one belongs to the large house-door; this, to the suite of rooms occupied by the councillor of blessed memory; and this, to the apartments which the councillor's wife inhabited. This key belongs to the young count's rooms; or,' continued he, rather embarrassed, 'to the rooms in the western wing, which belonged to your grandfather, Herr Count, when he was a young man.'

'Enough, good sir. We shall find our way,' said the count, as he smilingly interrupted him.

We approached the castle. 'Did you hear,' said the count, '*the young count's rooms?*' The young count was my grandfather. This shows that traditions never grow old. He is still called THE YOUNG COUNT here, although it is about fifty years since he died, old and infirm.'

As we entered the lofty arched entrance-hall, a

chill, dank air met us. Here and there a portion of the ornamental gilding from the walls had fallen away, and several large oil-paintings, representing bear-hunts, had become spotted with mould and dust.

'The entrance-hall is not particularly inviting,' said the count; 'but let us proceed farther.'

The key was placed into the heavy, elaborately ornamented door, leading to the apartments of the councillor above mentioned. We entered an antechamber, hung with several portraits and landscapes of the Dutch school; here, in a richly-gilt frame, which the hand of time had partially robbed of its brilliancy, was a lady dressed as a shepherdess, with a broad-brimmed straw hat upon her powdered head, and a shepherd's crook in her hand; a lovely smile played round the rosy lips, and the bright and speaking eyes sparkled with gaiety.

'That,' said the count, 'is my grandmother. She is smiling to us. She was painted as a bride, and there she still sits in her youthful beauty. It is the same with portraits as with the soul—they never grow old.'

We went on, and entered a room with a polished oaken floor, and the walls hung with gilded leather in richly-gilt partitions; there was a stiff grandeur about the room, which was rendered more formal by the old-fashioned furniture. The mouldings of the ceilings were decorated by groups of clumsy figures, a remnant of the grotesque taste, and accumulation of ornaments so prevalent in the seventeenth century. This had formerly been the chamber in which the councillor had studied, and it had been left untouched, just as it was during his lifetime. A clock, in a large stand of Chinese painting, in black and gold, stood silent and covered with dust in a corner, and a thick bell-rope with ponderous silk tassels still hung in another corner near the heavy writing-table, before which was placed, as if the student had only a moment before arisen from it, a narrow, high-backed chair, with legs curved outwards. Beyond this room came a bed-chamber, decorated in the style as the one we had just left.

'By Heavens,' said the count, 'it almost seems as if you were right. I cannot reconcile myself to these rooms, and to this furniture. Rooms and furniture—if I may so express myself—are our nearest acquaintances—a chair, a table, a sofa, are often our most intimate companions.'

At length we arrived at two small rooms, the

windows of which looked out upon the garden; they seemed to have been more recently occupied, and were more simply furnished.

'I shall pitch my tent here!' said the count. 'The arrangements cannot be said to be of the newest fashion, but, at any rate, there is a more cheerful aspect about this place than in any other part of the castle.'

Before the table stood an arm-chair, which formerly had been gilded, but now the white grounding was visible in many places; the red velvet with which it was covered was not faded; indeed, upon the whole, the colours were better preserved in this room than in the others. I was surprised at it, but the count, who regarded everything in his own peculiar way, merely remarked that the chamber lay on the northern side of the house.

'You see, Herr Pastor, where the full glare of the sun cannot penetrate, anything old is better preserved. It is a well-known fact, that what is ancient is best preserved in darkness; this holds good as well in the material as in the moral world, for light is only required by that which is growing. Objects that decay are more easily destroyed in light than in twilight. Hence,' he added, with a satirical curl of his lip, 'darkness is so necessary for the preservation of what is old.'

These apartments having been brought into some sort of order, the count established himself in them; from the time he had taken possession of his paternal property, his temper appeared to have become more equable. The castle harmonized with his restless soul, which cared not for the present, but loved rather to live amidst the memory of the past, which was crowded with familiar acquaintances; or, to endeavour to seek a dark and mysterious intercourse with another and to us unknown, world.

He was a visionary, but a noble visionary, with a deep sense of everything that is good and grand. I frequently visited him, and found him often engaged in reading, but he always hid his book when I entered. Once, however, I happened to catch a glimpse of it; it was Jung Stilling's works.

'I see, count,' said I, 'that you are reading about ghosts and apparitions. You surely do not believe in them?'

'Why should I not? Is there anything absurd in that belief, or do you suppose that man is the only being in the creation intellectually endowed? That *he* stands next to God? Do you not believe in the possibility that the human soul, when freed from its vile earthly garment, can receive a more perfect, an ethereal body, suited to its new state? *I* believe in it, and find comfort in the thought. What were man if he did not, even here below, penetrate, however dimly, into a future existence, and acquire a slight knowledge of its mysteries? What were we did we not all believe in this, to a greater or lesser extent? I maintain that there does not exist a man who has not some belief in spirits, even though he may ridicule the idea to others. When Death steals away the best beloved of a man's heart, seizes her in his bony arms, and draws her down into the gloom of the grave—when the hand of Providence lies heavily upon him—rest assured, my friend, *that* man will believe in a spiritual world.'

'Assuredly; and he ought to do so. No one should dare to doubt the future existence of the soul.'

'I speak of the atmosphere as being peopled with spirits; to that belief the soul of man clings when sorrowing for the dead.'

'Sorrow often leads to wild ideas,' I remarked.

'Sorrow!' repeated the count. 'You are partly

right; sorrow constitutes the night in the fate of mankind. When we are prosperous we heed not the noiseless, measured movement of the wheel of fate; the earthy element asserts its right over us, and cheats us into the belief that we are happy. True happiness and sorrow are more in unison than we are apt to fancy. If we sit on a peaceful evening with a beloved wife and her children, and thank the Lord for all the blessings we enjoy, it is their presence which constitutes our happiness; or, if we fall upon our knees by the side of their inanimate corpses, though we are bowed down with grief for their loss at first, after a time we cease to feel that we are alone. There is a something invisible, inaudible, and yet intelligible to our inmost soul that tells us restoration succeeds to dissolution, and life succeeds to death; and this something I call a mysterious intercourse with the spirit world.'

'But, count,' I suggested, 'reason points out to us—'

'Reason!' repeated he, impetuously interrupting me. 'Speak not of cold reason! What is that power which some possess of divining every feeling, every thought of those near them? What is feeling in comparison with foreboding—judgment in comparison with faith? He who acknowledges the existence of a higher world—who sincerely and earnestly believes in a connection between his feelings and their author—God—is a person of elevated mind; the man, on the contrary, who in his pride of intellect detracts from the Holy One, and divides the indivisible, is grovelling and limited in his ideas. I never could endure that over-wise reason, which would force itself into everything, fancying that it could take part in everything, without doing so in reality. Do not say, therefore, Herr Pastor, what reason points out to us. I contend that reason knows nothing about the matter.'

I found it was not worth while to dispute with the count, for as he would not admit the right of reason, I had nothing to advance against his vague and undefinable notions.

'It is a comfort,' said the count, one day, 'to believe in spiritual visits. I live alone here; my servants inhabit the second story, and you may possibly fancy that my time often hangs heavily on my hands. Far from it; when my candles begin to burn dimly in the evening, and the thick foliage is rustling gently—when the old furniture creaks, and a distant sound is heard, which may either be taken for the ringing of bells or the chanting of low murmuring voices, then my true life begins. I saunter up and down the room, and at times stand still and listen. Ah, then, often do I feel as if a flood of joy were rushing on my wounded heart — there is a flitting sound in the adjoining chamber— " Julia, Julia! thou hast not forgotten me!" I exclaim; and, calm and happy, I retire to rest and fall asleep dreaming of her.'

The count sank into deep thought, but he soon raised his dark eyes again, and gazing into my face, he said,

'You are my friend, are you not, even though you do not approve of my chimeras, as you reasonable people call them? I speak of my Julia; you do not know her, although she has for year belonged to your parish. She it was who, on the evening that I saw you for the first time, was conveyed to her last resting-place—she, my wife. I will tell you about my Julia, and you must not endeavour to dissuade me, by reasoning, from a belief which has become so necessary to me.'

The count seated himself in a large arm-chair, and began his narrative as follows:

The house of Baron Lindesparre, in Stockholm, was, at the period from which my story dates, the rendezvous of all the talent and beauty of the capital. His soirées were noted for the distinguished tone which pervaded them, for their unconstrained mirth, and their elegance without ostentation. His splendid apartments were tastefully arranged, without a single article being placed so as to appear more prominent than the rest: where all was luxury the profusion was not observable. It was only when one analyzed the magnificence of the house that one found it *was* magnificent.

The baron had been many years a widower: his wife, a Spaniard by birth, I never saw, but she had left a daughter, beautiful and gentle, a being formed partly of the glowing roses of the South, and partly of the snow of the North. She was the fairy of the place, and hundreds vied for a smile from her lips. This was Julia. She became my wife.

We had been married half a year, and had a separate residence, but on every soirée Julia went to her father's to do the honours of the house. On one of these evenings the company was more numerous than usual, and I observed a gentleman among the crowd whom I did not know, and who kept his eyes continually fixed upon my wife. He was tall and thin, with a countenance pale and attenuated, the features were almost stiff and inanimate, and the flashing eyes alone, which he fixed with a sort of scornful look upon my Julia, betrayed life. He was dressed in black, but a small star of brilliants sparkled from his button-hole, showing that he was in the service of some government. The man appeared to be about fifty years of ago, and a few grey hairs peeped out here and there among his otherwise black locks. I know not why I took such a strong interest in him; I fancied him disagreeable, and yet I was attracted to him. His was a sort of spell such as certain snakes are said to exercise over their victims.

My father-in-law came towards me. 'Who is that gentleman dressed in black?' I asked.

'Ah,' answered the old man, 'I had almost forgotten to introduce you; he is a Spaniard, a countryman of my beloved wife. Come.'

I followed him, and soon stood before the strange-looking guest.

'Don Caldero,' began my father-in-law; 'allow me to have the honour of introducing to you my son-in-law, Count Lejonswärd—Don Caldero, attaché to the Spanish Embassy.'

The stranger in the black dress said a few polite words to my father-in-law, who then moved on.

'As far as I can judge from observation, count, you are the happiest husband in all cold Sweden. I am glad to have made your acquaintance,' said the Spaniard; 'I have long remarked you, and intended to have inquired your name. You, like myself, appear to pay attention not only to the outward but also to the inward properties of mankind. I rejoice to have met a kindred spirit.'

Thus began my acquaintance with a man who, notwithstanding his cold, severe, repulsive manners, possessed a fiery soul, and a mind capable of conceiving grand ideas. From this evening Don Caldero became intimate with me, and his clear understanding, the captivating warmth which he too well knew how to mingle with his elegant conversation, guided my ideas and feelings into a direction for which I was already predisposed by character, but in which, without Don Caldero, I probably never would have gone so far. He often visited at our house, and I became more and more attached to the highly-talented and well-informed Spaniard, and he, too, seemed disposed to like me. It was he who, with a clearness which I am not capable of imitating, pointed out to me the connection between God and man, between the visible and the invisible world; who proved to me the existence of a communication between a spiritual world and ours, manifested in dreams, forebodings, and in mysterious intimations of the influence of a higher power, which we experience in moments of grave importance. It was he who placed before me the truth of apparitions, purified from all superstition—that is to say, denying them to be gross, material manifestations, but receiving them as produced through the interposition of beings endowed with greater powers of intellect than ourselves. You should have heard him, sir, and though you are so great a sceptic, you would have believed him as I did.

We often amused ourselves with playing at chess, game that has always interested me greatly. Don Caldero shared my taste, and we sometimes fought a whole evening over one game.

'Chess pleases me,' he used to say, 'because it depends less than anything else upon the chance of fate. Fate makes itself visible everywhere, hence one must seek a pastime which excludes it as much as possible; our pastimes ought to be such, that spirits cannot interfere and amuse themselves at our expense.'

Don Caldero frequented my father-in-law's soirées, and my house, but hitherto he had never invited me to visit him. He resided in a large mansion quite by himself, and never received any strangers. His character did not attract people, it rather caused him to be avoided; for few knew, or could understand, his great worth, and fewer still were inclined to follow him in his bold flights through the vast regions of fancy.

After praising his friend at some length, the count concluded his eulogy by saying:

In a word, Herr Pastor, there is but one such man in the world, and that man is called Caldero.

At length, one evening, Caldero *did* invite me. He lived at the farther end of the northern suburb, in a house which he had furnished according to his own taste. On entering the saloon I found no one, the apartment was empty, and merely lighted by a single handsome lamp, which hung from the ceiling, and which cast a subdued light around. I went farther: everywhere I encountered the same silence, the same twilight, the same heavy grandeur, which was to be traced in every object. I stood still, a strange feeling creeping over me, the nursery legends about enchanted castles flashed across my mind, and I fancied myself transported into one whose owner, with all his retainers, lay in one of the inner chambers, buried for many centuries in a profound magical slumber. These thoughts were soon, however, chased away by soft steps upon the rich carpet, and Caldero's gloomy figure stood before me.

'Welcome, count!' he said, courteously. 'I thank you for coming to my hermitage, where, you must know, I have never invited anyone but yourself. I longed for one evening to take entire possession of you; pardon my selfishness.'

He led me into the inner cabinet. This was a small chamber, but lofty, and fitted up in a still more gloomy style than the others. The walls, hung with dark-red velvet, contrasted strangely with the white and gold pilasters which stood at the four corners. In the middle of the room was a table, upon which was placed a chessboard between a pair of tall wax candles. We seated ourselves upon the sofa, and my host appeared to be reflecting upon something; at length he exclaimed:

'Count! perhaps you may think it extraordinary that the Spaniard Caldero has formed such an affection for you. He considers it his duty to explain why; but in order to do so, I must give you a slight sketch of my history.'

I listened with great attention to what this strange introduction might lead, and Don Caldero continued:

'I was born and educated in Madrid; my father was a poor but excellent man, belonging to the ancient nobility, and I imbibed from my earliest infancy high notions of the value of rank. Latterly it has fallen in my estimation, although I cannot even now entirely free myself from a prejudice in favour of the advantages of good birth. I was, as I said before, poor, but proud, as every Spaniard should be, and an ardent longing to obtain honour and distinction dwelt in my youthful breast. This longing was increased tenfold by my passion for a lovely girl as poor as myself, but even more richly endowed with ancestors. The slight difference which existed in the ancientness of our lineage, combined with my poverty, prevented our love from becoming anything more than a hopeless passion; for her parents, proud of their pure Christian blood, which for centuries had remained unmixed, could not endure the idea of their daughter uniting herself to me, whose early ancestor was a Moor, a scion of that noble race who once occupied a portion of Spain. Still youth and love easily forget these small differences, and Maria, so the young lady was called, loved me most fervently. Often when she left mass she bestowed upon me a few minutes undisturbed by witnesses. Ah! how happy I then was! I fancied my own individual merit would, in time, convince Maria's parents that I was worthy of her hand; I therefore sought to be appointed to the diplomatic corps, a path which, under our weak government, was a sure road to distinction; nor was it long before I was named attaché to the mission to Vienna.

'I met my beloved; it was for the last time; and never shall that moment pass from my memory.

'"Do not forget your faithful Alphonso," I whispered, as I pressed her in my arms. I felt how her tears rolled down her blooming cheeks.

'"See, beloved Maria," I said, at length, giving her a small golden chain, which I had received from my mother—"see, here is something as a remembrance of me; keep it faithfully. If, however, you should forsake me, then return it to me, and I will wear it, and die thinking of, and praying for, you."'

'"Never, never!" murmured Maria, as she took the chain.

'"Never, never!" I repeated, pressing her to my heart. "But, Maria!" I continued after I had become more composed, "you might perhaps, forget me; will you, as a proof of our eternal union, share a consecrated wafer with your lover?" I had one, which I broke in two. "God is our witness!" we both said. The clock in the adjoining cloister struck eleven.

'"I must go," cried Maria. "For ever yours; for ever and for ever!"

'Long after she had disappeared I stood rooted to the spot, striving to catch a glimpse of her in the moonlight. "For ever—for ever!" sounded in my ears, and, midst golden dreams of a future full of bliss and honour, I wended my way home.

'I had been about a year in Vienna, when one evening a stranger brought me a packet. It contained the chain. I was horrified.

'"Deceived!—forsaken!—forgotten!" I cried.

"But no, it is impossible!" A slip of paper which was enclosed, contained, to my comfort, the following words: "I remember my oath, but am *forced* to break it. Do not despise Maria."'

Don Caldero showed me a locket, which he wore near his heart. 'Do you know this face?' said he. I started; they were the features of my wife.

'My wife!' I cried, in an agitated voice.

'No, my friend,' replied Caldero, with a bitter smile; 'it was her mother. On this account I attached myself to you, for I still love the mother in her child. I have suffered, I have become resigned, but I have never *forgotten:* and I willingly cling to the belief, that necessity and compulsion alone robbed me of my Maria. Let us play, count.'

I silently seated myself at the chess-table, on which was ranged a splendid set of chessmen; the board was of black-and-white stone, and the men of one party were of silver, with tops of clear crystal, diamond cut, while those of the other side were of a dark steel-coloured metal, with dark red-tops.

'It is not usual,' began Don Caldero, 'to play chess for money; yet why should we not at least venture something? I should like—I have often very strange ideas—I should like to give your Julia the chain which her mother possessed for a time; it is neither valuable nor modern, but perhaps if she hears its history, she may kindly wear it in remembrance of Don Caldero. I will stake the necklace, and you, count, will you stake a lock of the dark hair of your Julia? She will doubtless give it, if you ask for it. You must forgive an old, despised lover, for fancying he sees the mother when he gazes on your wife.'

'I consent willingly to this arrangement,' I replied, smiling.

We played; but it seemed as though Don Caldero took pains to lose, and he speedily succeeded in his endeavours.

'I am vanquished,' he said quietly, as he went towards a casket, which I had not hitherto observed. 'Here, count, is the chain; I shall be more calm when it is no longer in my hands.'

The chain was more costly than I had imagined, and I was pleased at the idea of Julia wearing it when Caldero visited us. I instantly wrote a note to Julia, in which, without mentioning anything about her mother, I told her of Caldero's and my bet, and begged her for a lock of her hair, in case, against my expectation, I should lose the next game. I sent a servant to my house with this note and the chain to my wife, after which we again returned to the chess-table. Now Caldero became more cautious; I, on the contrary, was seized by a secret anxiety, an uneasiness which I could not explain. I did not perceive the false moves I was too evidently making. Don Caldero drew my attention to my carelessness and more than once, made me take back my move; all was in vain, I was as though bewitched, and could no longer calculate my position. At length the servant returned, bringing a small note from Julia. She jested at the taste of our Spanish friend, yet sent the lock of hair, at the same time entreating me not again, not even for more costly ornaments than the chain, to stake the ringlets of my wife. I showed Caldero the note; he read it, and seemed to turn pale.

'Her handwriting resembles her mother's,' he said, and laid the note upon the table. 'Let us continue.'

We played on, but I soon found myself completely surrounded by his men; my strange uneasiness increased at each moment; I felt as though a drawn sword were suspended by a hair over my head; the candles seemed to burn blue; the white tops of my kings appeared to assume a pale milk-white colour, whereas the dark-red of Caldero's men glowed like fiery coals, radiant with some inward light.

'Checkmated,' he said, in a low tone. 'Checkmated, count,' he repeated, louder; but I sat immovable, staring fixedly at the chessmen. I experienced a horrible sensation, as though an evil spirit were standing behind me, with his burning hot hand upon my head; nevertheless I was shivering—a death-like coldness had crept over my whole body, and yet—At length I ventured to glance at Don Caldero; his gloomy countenance was more pale than usual, he looked like a corpse, and his dark hollow eyes were intently fixed upon me. 'This is the 12th of August,' he murmured, as if to himself. 'Reconciliation with the dead. Count, give me the lock of hair.'

I handed it to him, and then, rising from my seat as one intoxicated, I staggered out of the house. I was conscious of nothing that was going on; but Caldero followed me.

'Forgive me, count, my strange behaviour; but it is exactly twenty years this day since Maria and I shared the consecrated wafer. I have kept my oath. Good night, count. Do not forget your friend.'

I hastened home. Never in my life have I so distinctly heard a voice of warning in the inmost depths of my soul. 'Hasten! hasten! hasten!' cried the voice; and I flew rather than walked.

'Is Julia up still?' I asked of the servant who let me in.

'The countess?' he inquired.

'Yes, yes; the countess!'

'The countess must be still up; she dismissed her maid only a few minutes ago.'

I ran to my wife's room. Julia was sitting in an arm-chair before her toilet-table, and quite calmly, as though she had not heard my hasty steps.

'God be praised that my foreboding of evil has not proved true!' I exclaimed.

No answer.

'Julia!' I cried, in an agony of anxiety—'Julia, do you not hear me?'

Still the same silence. She sat immovable before the mirror, and her lovely features were reflected in the glass; the trinket which I had won was round her neck, and a gentle expression was in her tender black eyes.

'Julia! Julia!' I cried, seizing her hand. It was cold, but not rigid. God! my God! She was dead! I know not what further happened, but a fortnight later I was with you, Herr Pastor, to place the remains of my Julia in my family vault.'

The count had risen, and strode up and down the room in great agitation. The clock struck eleven.

'Art thou there, Julia?' he cried, while his eyes roved wildly round. 'Come in! come in!' He opened the door leading to the adjoining room, and called out into the darkness, 'Julia, I am here! here is thy husband!' A cold draught of air alone was wafted into the room, and a slight rustling noise was discernible. 'She passes on,' said the count. He slammed the door, and sank into an arm-chair. 'She will not come to me! My God! my God! let me go to her!'

The count sat for awhile lost in deep thought; at length he sprang up, gazed at me with eyes beaming with joy, and exclaimed.

'Pastor Z., it is glorious to hope!'

When I left him I actually found myself trembling, and I was right glad that the servant lighted me along the deserted apartments, so powerful is the effect of the imagination when excited.

I continued to visit the count from time to time. His grief had, I fancied, calmed down, but his health was beginning to suffer, imperceptibly to himself perhaps, but not so to those who saw him now and then. I remarked that he was gradually becoming more strange; he often laughed at things which were not at all ludicrous; nevertheless, he was always the same amiable man I had ever known him, and his judgment was clear on every subject except when the mystic world was touched upon, then his thoughts used to wander, and Julia, his beloved Julia, was always the pivot round which his ideas turned.

In the middle of winter I suddenly received a message, to the effect that I was wanted immediately at the castle. The messenger could not tell the reason why I had been summoned, but said that the count's valet had ordered him to saddle a horse and to ride as fast as he could to me. I suspected some misfortune, so set off instantly.

When I entered the count's room he was seated at a table.

'Ah, is it you, Pastor Z.?' he said, when he perceived me. 'Have you come to preach peace to my soul? Begin, sir; it will be amusing to listen—

ha, ha, ha!—to hope in God? God? what is that? No, pastor, now I am wise—I believe in nothing, not even in myself, nor in you, priest, you black-skinned slug! You are one of those who wind themselves round mankind, and lie with a double tongue! Speak on, sir!'

His flashing eyes and uplifted arm, which threatened to strike, caused me to start back: he was evidently deranged. His pale lips trembled with rage, and his black hair hung in disorder about his brow, from which drops of perspiration rolled down his cheeks. I perceived that here I could be of no use; I therefore went to the bell to summon the servant. He made his appearance, pale, and with eyes red from weeping.

'Look!' cried the count, wildly laughing—'only look, Pastor Z.! The livelong night he has been borrowing from the fountain of tears, and talking no end of nonsense, merely because I told the fool the simple fact that neither he nor I possessed a soul, and that there is no such thing as right or wrong. Well? How comical you look—ha, ha, ha! You, and my man yonder, look like a couple of frightened sheep. You may rely on what I say, he would have come if it had been in his power; but all is over, he cannot come. Yes, look yonder, stare at your heaven: it is air, mere air, nothing but empty air. Do you understand? The earth is a solid lump, upon which cabbages, long-tailed monkeys, men, and other plants grow; and above is heaven, that is to say, sensibly speaking, air, atmosphere. Well? Are you not capable of comprehending this? it is as clear as the day. Just listen,' he continued; 'mankind is a sort of animal of prey, which, even when tamed, do not lose their natural propensities; they are worse than beasts of prey, for even the tiger loves its mate and its young, but look, man murders them—murders, do you hear?'

He hid his face in his hands, and wept aloud.

'I do not know what the letter could have contained,' whispered the servant. 'The count received it yesterday evening; he seemed overjoyed when he beheld the handwriting, and before I left the room; when I returned, however, he was just as you now see him. The poor count!' he continued; 'he was such an excellent master!'

The count sprang to his feet as if he had been terrified by something. 'Ho!' he cried, and his wild eyes wandered round the room. 'So much blood, so much poison were flowing over the earth; then a serpent stretched out its scaly head from the bottomless pit and seized the white dove. She fluttered her wings, the poor little thing, but first one part of her and then the other was crushed in the serpent's throat. It was her dead mother who devoured her: it was horrible! Look yonder— look, Herr Pastor! A thick darkness overspread the earth; not a single ray of hope could penetrate through the bloody vapour to her! Nay, good pastor, it was merely a freak of fancy, but at the same time a picture of the truth. Her mother and her husband murdered her. Do you *now* understand?'

In this strain the unhappy man continued to rave for several days. I remained in the castle, for I hoped he might rally. A doctor was called in: he applied many remedies, none of which, however, seemed to afford the sufferer any relief. The count continued to be insane, and never for an instant did he close his eyes in sleep. At length, however, he became exhausted, and was obliged to be carried to his bed. I was then called to him. How much he had changed! his dark eyes had sunken greatly, and looked like flames half extinguished; his cheeks had fallen in, and his brow was full of wrinkles. He lay apparently in a state of complete exhaustion, and when I addressed him he did not answer.

His servant privately handed me the fatal letter. It was from Don Caldero, and ran as follows:

'Dear Count,—When this letter reaches you, I shall be no more. It shall be laid in my desk, ready to be sent to you after my death. I owe you an explanation to divest you of your erroneous ideas respecting another world. For a long time past I have not believed in a future life, but it has been one of my favourite amusements to observe the faith of enthusiasts. It gave me pleasure when I perceived a man misled by his faith, and I laughed in my sleeve at such folly. I influenced your opinions, as I found you to be a fit subject for my experiments.

'I am a Catholic; from my youth upwards my eye has been accustomed to weeping Madonnas; I have heard the miracles respecting the saints narrated, and was expected to believe all I heard. The consequence is, that I have ended by believing nothing, The whole of religion rests upon the conviction of the present and eternal existence of the immortal soul; but there is no proof that man possesses a soul, any more than there is proof of the truth of the above-mentioned miracles. Man is an animal like the other inhabitants of the globe, with this exception only, that he has a more perfectly-developed brain, and a greater number of intellectual organs. Life is quite independent of soul. I have studied these subjects, and have become convinced that the theory about the soul is a fabrication of the priesthood, invented to enable them the more easily to govern the body. There can be no Divine disposer of human events, else wickedness would not prosper in this world as it does, whilst uprightness suffers. There is a governing law in nature which dooms mankind to death, just as the trees are compelled annually to shed their leaves. I saw how oaths were broken with impunity; I shared with a maiden, whom I loved more than my life, a consecrated wafer, the most sacred thing I then knew: *she* broke the oath and became happy, while *I*, who kept it, became miserable. Hence I began to believe in fate, and not in Providence, and learned to despise mankind to prevent myself from hating them.

'I met you and your Julia; she was *her* daughter. She was beautiful, and as yet nothing had occurred to try her character. For awhile my old dreams of faithful love revived, and for the daughter's sake I forgave the mother, who had so deeply wounded the most sacred of all feelings, if anything *can* be termed sacred. To be brief, count, I fancied myself once more in my enthusiastic youthful days; I forgot the sentiments experience had induced me to adopt, and faith in Maria's love blossomed anew in my heart, like the flowers which take root in the loose ashes of a volcano. I fancied my innocent Maria would meet me in another world with a kind welcome, and joyfully traverse with me the regions of space. You see, count, that the notion of eternity and God proceeds from our conceptions of love, and that, where there is no love, faith is also wanting.

'Your wife died suddenly on the anniversary of the day on which Maria and I had taken the oath. I considered this event as a sign from Heaven, from her who, yonder above the skies, still loved me. I thought the mother had called her daughter to herself, for she was the only being on earth who testified to her broken oath. I deceived myself.

'I had scarcely returned to Spain, when I received a visit from a monk.

'"Pardon me, señor," said he, "if I take the

liberty of putting a question to you. Have you a chain, which you once received from a distinguished lady whom you loved?"

' I gazed at the man in astonishment, and answered, " Yes; what can you know about it?"

' " Señor, I prepared an old woman for death who had been engaged in some cases of poisoning, and she confessed the following, which she gave me permission to repeat, if by so doing any advantage might be gained: 'One evening,' these were her words, 'I was summoned to a young and beautiful lady, she was called Maria Viso'—was that the name of your beloved?—'and she begged me to insert a powerful poison in the clasp of a chain.'

' " Although the wretched woman was accustomed to such commissions, she nevertheless asked who was to wear the chain? The lady answered that it had been given to her by an importunate suitor who was called Caldero, and she now wished to send back the chain to him. She also said that her feelings towards him were changed, and she now preferred another, but that her parents, who formerly opposed her marriage with him, had become anxious for it, and wished to force it on her, and she was determined to get rid of him.

'" The woman thereupon inserted the poison into the clasp. The lady had afterwards married a heretic, and this act of hers it was which had roused the poisoner's conscience, for notwithstanding her being so great a criminal, she was an orthodox Catholic. She sought to find you out, in the hope that the scheme had not succeeded according to the lady's intentions. The Lord be praised and thanked that you did not wear that chain, you would undoubtedly have died if you had; the best thing you can do with it will be to present it to our poor monastery, for with the pure everything is pure, and the poison might be expunged by melting the gold."

'I stood like one turned into a statue of stone. It was, then, the decree of fate that the mother should be accessary to the daughter's death, and the latter be sacrificed for the crime of the former!

'Picture to yourself now, if you can, count, blessed spirits : imagine to yourself, now, a heaven on earth with a woman you love; cling to a belief in another world; if you can do all this, then you are indeed a perfect fool. I have relapsed into my old views: the earth remains earth, and nothing more. When you are reading this I shall be dead, cold, and buried. If, however, I have an immortal soul, you will know the contents of this letter before it arrives, otherwise you must believe that nothing remains of him who once was your friend.

'CALDERO.'

The much-to-be-pitied victim of Caldero's cold atheism and contempt of mankind still sat in the same position, staring gloomily before him, without uttering a syllable, but now and then heaving a deep-drawn sigh. It was evident that he would soon be at rest, for every day he became weaker and weaker.

I scarcely ever left the bedside of the unfortunate young man, in the hope that he might, if only for a few minutes, regain his senses, when I could speak peace to his soul.

One evening, after this sad state of affairs had continued without interruption for a fortnight, I was sitting at a table reading, with my back turned to the count, when I heard a low whispering behind me; it was his voice. I listened—it was a fervent, humble prayer for peace in death, and pardon for all his sins. I let him finish his prayer undisturbed.

'Who is there?' asked the count, in a feeble tone.

I drew near to the bed.

'Is it you, Pastor Z.?' he said mildly. 'Still up? It is late. I am happy now, my friend, for it will soon be day; I have had a long night. I am dying, but I hear within me a strong voice crying, 'Love is faith,' and I pray, bowing myself in humility before the God of Love. I have wandered from the right path, I was misled, misfortune pursued me, and I became, through my thoughtlessness, Julia's murderer. The crushing intelligence contained in Caldero's letter shook my trust in everything, for it is a relief to a guilty soul not to believe in a Judge. But my presumptuous folly was punished, my understanding became obscured. A light has burst upon me now, and since I have prayed I feel at peace. I prayed—for many years I neglected to do so—yes, I prayed with clasped hands, as my mother used to teach me when I was an innocent child. Alas, I ought always to have prayed thus.'

He ceased speaking, and leaning his head against his pillow, he looked steadfastly at me with a mild, glorified expression of countenance. I had sunk upon my knees at the side of his bed, and poured forth thanks to my God for the ray of light and hope which he had permitted to penetrate the darkened mind of the poor sufferer.

'Lord!' I entreated, 'grant him light!'

'Light,' he repeated, in a low whisper, 'Lord! more light. God be praised! there *is* light!'

He closed his eyes, heaved a long sigh, and in another world he received an explanation of that secret, the solution of which he had only grasped in his last hour.

He now reposes in the family vault by the side of his beloved Julia; the receptacle of the dead is full. The pieces of his shattered escutcheon lie scattered upon the floor around his coffin,[*] and the key of the vault will be needed no more!

[*] At the death of the last representative of a noble family in Sweden, the escutcheon is usually broken over his coffin.

END OF VOL. II.

LONDON : PRINTED BY W. CLOWES AND SONS, STAMFORD STREET, AND CHARING CROSS.

www.ingramcontent.com/pod-product-compliance
Lightning Source LLC
Chambersburg PA
CBHW030815230426
43667CB00008B/1233